THE CARTOON GUIDE TO

ECONOMICS

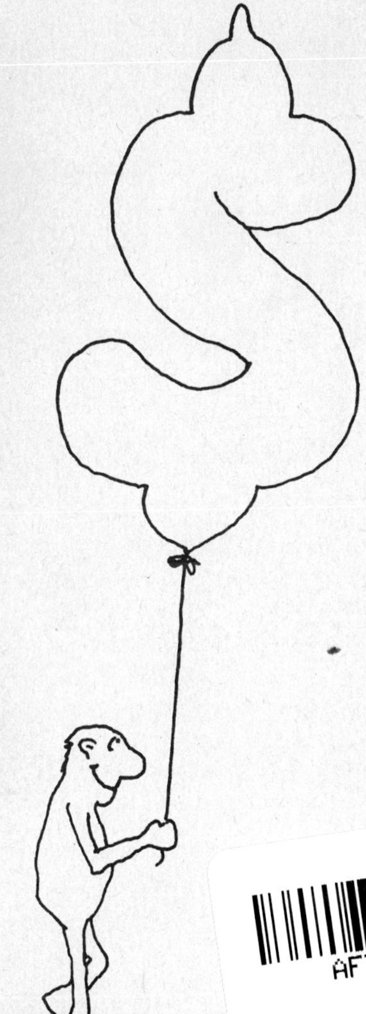

POP

THE CARTOON GUIDE TO
ECONOMICS

by Douglas Michael

BARNES & NOBLE BOOKS
A DIVISION OF HARPER & ROW, PUBLISHERS
New York, Cambridge, Philadelphia
San Francisco, London, Mexico City
São Paulo, Singapore, Sydney

For George R.
"Sometime Travel Companion"

 For information address Harper & Row, Publishers, Inc., 10 East 53rd Street, New York, N.Y. 10022. Published simultaneously in Canada by Fitzhenry & Whiteside Limited, Toronto.

FIRST EDITION

Library of Congress Cataloging-in-Publication Data

Michael, Douglas.
The cartoon guide to economics.

Bibliography: p.
Includes index.
1. Economics—Caricatures and cartoons. I. Title.
HB75.M48 1985 330'.0207 84-48612
ISBN 0-06-460419-5 (pbk.)

85 86 87 88 89 MPC 10 9 8 7 6 5 4 3 2 1

CONTENTS

POP

PART 1

ECONOMICS AND THE SEARCH FOR PROSPERITY

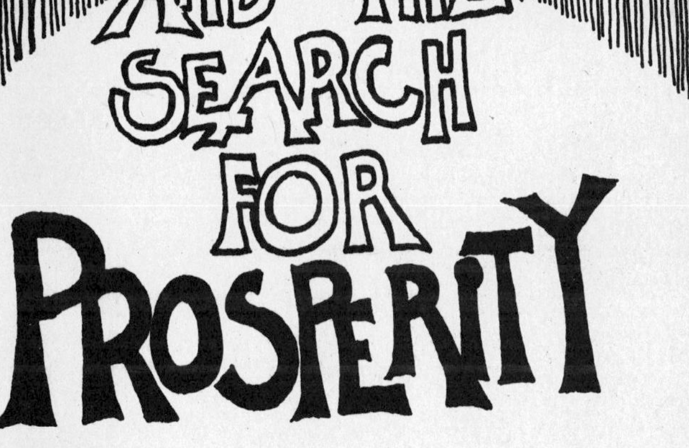

THE STONE AGE. SO NAMED FOR THE PREVAILING BELIEF THAT **PROSPERITY** WAS BUT A MERE **'STONE'S THROW'** AWAY.

UNFORTUNATELY, BEHIND EVERY PROMISE OF PROSPERITY... DOOM, DEPRESSION AND DESPAIR INVARIABLY REARED THEIR UGLY HEADS.
FOR STONE AGERS, THIS PRIMITIVE STYLE 'BOOM & BUST' ECONOMY SEEMED TO OFFER LITTLE HOPE FOR REAL PROSPERITY.

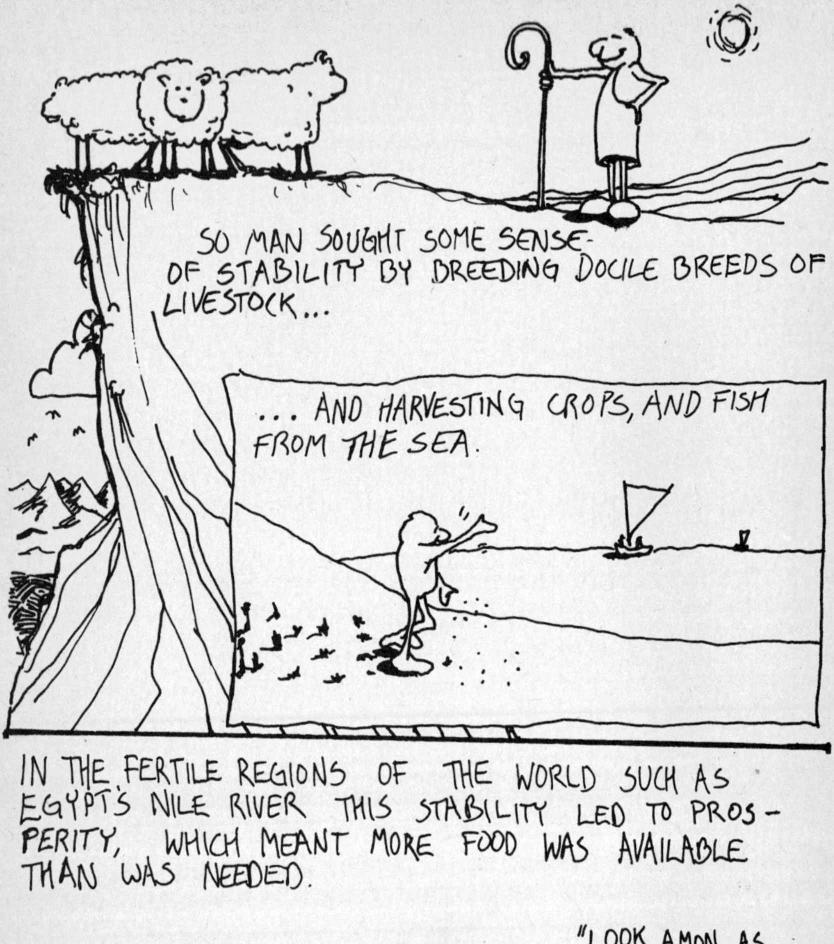

IN THE FERTILE REGIONS OF THE WORLD SUCH AS EGYPT'S NILE RIVER THIS STABILITY LED TO PROSPERITY, WHICH MEANT MORE FOOD WAS AVAILABLE THAN WAS NEEDED.

OUT OF THESE RANKS CAME THE **PHARAOHS** AND **KINGS** WHO ORGANIZED THEIR SOCIETIES INTO WHAT ARE KNOWN AS **COMMAND** ECONOMIES. THAT IS, ONE PERSON, OR A FEW, DETERMINED WHAT JOBS WERE TO BE DONE, AND WHO WOULD DO THEM.

THE **COMMAND** ECONOMY SENT THOUSANDS OF MEN OFF TO CONSTRUCT SUCH GREAT TOURIST ATTRACTIONS OF THE FUTURE AS THE PYRAMIDS AND, IN LATER TIMES, THE GREAT WALL OF CHINA.

MEN PRESSED INTO SUCH CONSTRUCTION PROJECTS WERE TYPICALLY OUT-OF-TOWNERS WITH ONLY ONE HOPE FOR RETIREMENT.

THESE HARD LESSONS WERE NOT LOST ON THE HOMETOWN FOLKS WHO WERE OFTEN **HIRED** AS ARTISANS AND CRAFTSMEN - AND AS SUCH DEVELOPED A TENDENCY TO KEEP SUCH VALUED SKILLS IN THE FAMILY.

FOR EXAMPLE, IN ANCIENT EGYPT A YOUNG MAN WAS THOUGHT TO COMMIT THE MOST HORRIBLE SACRILEGE IF HE WANTED TO CHANGE HIS OCCUPATION FROM THAT OF HIS FATHER'S.

WHAT BEGAN AS A **TENDENCY** TO PASS SKILLS DOWN FROM GENERATION TO GENERATION BECAME **RIGID LAW** ASSURING SOCIETY THAT ALL NEEDED TASKS WOULD BE PERFORMED. ORGANIZING SOCIETY IN THIS MANNER - WHERE EACH MAN IS BORN INTO HIS POSITION FOR LIFE - IS REFERRED TO AS A **TRADITIONAL** ECONOMY.

PEOPLE BEGAN TO TRADE... EXCHANGING THINGS THEY DIDN'T NEED OR HAD TOO MANY OF FOR THINGS THEY DIDN'T HAVE AND NEEDED. THIS WAS CALLED **BARTERING** AND IT BECAME THE BASIS OF FREE TRADE OR THE **MARKET** ECONOMY.

TRADE FREED PEOPLE FROM HAVING TO PROVIDE FOR THEMSELVES ALL THE NECESSITIES OF LIFE. BY BARTERING, EACH PERSON COULD **SPECIALIZE** AT ONE TASK, THEN TRADE THEIR SURPLUS WITH OTHERS TO OBTAIN THE THINGS THEY NEEDED. FINE. HOWEVER...

BARTERING DID PRESENT ONE PROBLEM...

ADDITIONAL 'LESSER KNOWN' COMPLICATIONS OF
BARTERING ~
...GAME SHOW PRIZES ALWAYS SEEMED TO LACK SOMETHING...
"O.K. LUCKY GUY, YOU CAN KEEP THE OLD TROJAN WARRIOR AND THE BARREL OF FISH, OR... YOU CAN GO FOR WHATEVER'S IN THAT CAULDRON THERE!"
TAKE THE CAULDRON!
...'TIPPING' WAS JUST TOO TOUGH TO FIGURE...
HEY! YA' COULDA' LEFT AN EGG OR SOMETHING!
EXIT
WALLETS AND PURSES WERE BULKY AND CUMBERSOME.
THIS IS GETTING RIDICULOUS.

UNFORTUNATELY, FOR MONEY TO HAVE VALUE IT MUST REQUIRE SOME EFFORT TO OBTAIN IT!

"THEM SHARKS THERE REQUIRE EFFORT TO GET AT... WHY DON'T WE USE THEM FOR MONEY?"
WELL, YES, SNARING A SHARK WOULD REQUIRE SOME EFFORT. BUT, IN ADDITION, MONEY MUST **MAINTAIN** ITS VALUE OVER TIME.
PHEW! GET RID OF IT!
FINE! THROW AWAY OUR LIFE'S SAVINGS!
BUT MOST IMPORTANTLY, FOR ANY SUBSTANCE TO WORK AS MONEY IT MUST BE **ACCEPTABLE** AS A MEDIUM OF EXCHANGE TO ALL MEMBERS OF A SOCIETY.
HERE YOU GO - ONE HOOF. THAT SHOULD DO IT.
HOOF! HOOF! FOR FIXING MY SANDAL.
NOW WAIT A MINUTE! WHAT'S THIS HOOF STUFF?
AW C'MON ITS GOOD - TAKE IT!
DIDN'T YOU SEE THE SIGN? WE DO NOT ACCEPT HOOFS.
HEY! I ACCEPTED IT. NOW YOU HAVE TO.
DONT WANT IT!
NO!

WHICH BRINGS US TO
GOLD & SILVER

NOTHING SEEMED BETTER SUITED FOR MONEY THAN THESE SCARCE METALS (GOLD & SILVER) IN COIN FORM. BY THE TIME ANCIENT GREECE WAS THRIVING THEIR ACCEPTANCE WAS WIDESPREAD. PEOPLE FOUND COINS CONVENIENT TO CARRY, CAPABLE OF HOLDING THEIR **VALUE** OVER TIME AND BEST OF ALL THEY COULD BE USED AS A **STANDARD** TO DETERMINE THE **VALUE** OF ANYTHING OFFERED FOR SALE. NEEDLESS TO SAY, ALL THIS TALK OF **VALUE** GOT THE EARLY GREEKS TO THINKING.

FOR THE PHILOSOPHERS, ECONOMICS POSED FEW QUESTIONS WORTH CONSIDERING. GREEK SOCIETY, FOR ALL ITS TALK OF DEMOCRACY AND IDEAL STATES, WAS STILL LARGELY A **COMMAND** SOCIETY WITH EASILY A THIRD OF THE POPULATION ENSLAVED.

TO ARISTOTLE SLAVERY WAS **NATURAL** - A MUTUAL BOND OF FRIENDSHIP AND COMMON INTEREST.

EVEN MORE INTERESTING WAS WHAT ARISTOTLE FOUND **UNNATURAL**. FOR INSTANCE, HE HAD A REAL PROBLEM WITH PEOPLE **BARTERING** OR **TRADING** THEIR GOODS FOR MONEY... AND AS FOR **USURY** - THE PRACTICE OF LENDING MONEY TO RECEIVE INTEREST - WELL...

THE PROBLEM WITH **TRADE**, TO ARISTOTLE, AROSE OVER THE QUESTION OF **VALUE**.

IF, FOR EXAMPLE, TWO PEOPLE EACH HAD AN ITEM FOR TRADE WHICH WAS **EQUAL** IN **VALUE** TO THE OTHER'S - THEN THERE WOULD BE NO INCENTIVE FOR TRADE. THEREFORE TRADE WOULD ONLY OCCUR WITH ITEMS **UNEQUAL** IN **VALUE**. AND THIS WOULD RESULT IN ONE MAN'S GAINING AT ANOTHER MAN'S EXPENSE.

AS FOR **USURY**, ARISTOTLE'S PROBLEM GREW OUT OF HIS **PERCEPTION** OF MONEY AS NOTHING MORE THAN A MEDIUM OF EXCHANGE. TO ARISTOTLE, MONEY WAS INCAPABLE OF INCREASING ITS VALUE BECAUSE IT WAS EMPTY OF VALUE IN ITSELF.

XENOPHON'S IDEA WAS SIMPLE IN THEORY, BUT IT GOT MESSY IN PRACTICE AS HISTORY WILL SHOW A LITTLE LATER ON.

ALTHOUGH ROME HAD A MORE COMPELLING LANDSCAPE, ROMAN AND GREEK ECONOMIES WERE ESSENTIALLY THE SAME.

WITH ONE EXCEPTION...

PROSPEROUS ROMANS THOUGHT MUCH MORE HIGHLY OF USURY THAN HAD THE GREEKS, AND AS SUCH THEY FORMALIZED THE PRACTICE AND BECAME THE WORLD'S FIRST BANKERS.

INDEED, ITALIANS BECAME SO FOND OF BANKING THAT WHEN THEIR EMPIRE CAME TO AN END, THE BANKING TRADITION REMAINED. AND WHILE THE REST OF EUROPE SLID INTO THE DARK AGES ITALIAN MERCHANT-BANK CITIES LIKE GENOA AND FLORENCE PROSPERED AND THRIVED.

FEUDALISM

WITH THE ROMAN EMPIRE NOW HISTORY, FEUDAL SOCIETY EMERGED AND SPREAD THROUGHOUT EUROPE. THESE WERE THE 'MIDDLE AGES,' A PERIOD OF HISTORY KNOWN MORE FOR ITS LENGTH THAN FOR ITS ENLIGHTENED THINKING.

FOR EXAMPLE:

THE HI-TECH TYPES OF THE DAY WERE ALL INTO ALCHEMY, THE CURIOUS SCIENCE OF TRANSFORMING JUST ABOUT ANYTHING INTO GOLD.

MEANWHILE MEDICAL SCIENCE WAS ADVANCING THE MOST PECULIAR IDEAS.

AS FOR SOCIAL SCRUCTURE FEUDALISM WAS, TO SAY THE LEAST, OPPRESSIVE.
PEASANTS HAD TO SWEAR ALLEGIANCE TO THEIR LORD AND SUBMIT TO HIS RULE...
I'D BE HONORED TO WORK YOUR LORDSHIP'S FIELD FOR THE MERE THRILL OF IT.
...AND LORDS, LIKEWISE TO THEIR KING...
...WHY MY PEASANTS AND I WOULD LOVE TO WAGE WAR TO OBTAIN A NICE DOWRY FOR YOUR DAUGHTER.
...AND CENTRAL TO IT ALL WAS THE CATHOLIC CHURCH, WHICH HAD THE ALLEGIANCE OF EVERYONE.
WE'LL WORK AND SUFFER ALL OUR LIVES IF IT MEANS YOU CAN GET US INTO HEAVEN.
YEA, AND I'LL GIVE YOU LAND AND PEASANTS AND WHATEVER ELSE YOU WANT IF YOU CAN GET ME INTO HEAVEN.
"QUE DOMINI QUE DOMINO"

AS FOR TRADE, THINGS WERE NOT SO GOOD. NEARLY EVERYONE DEVISED THEIR OWN SETS OF WEIGHTS AND MEASURES AND TO FURTHER COMPLICATE MATTERS, ONE OF THE MOST POPULAR SELF-EMPLOYMENTS OF THE DAY WAS OPERATING A TOLL BOOTH.

TO SAY THE LEAST, TIMES WERE STALE AND LIFE WAS STATIC. *HOWEVER*, SOMETHING CHANGED ALL THAT. THE HOLY CITY OF JERUSALEM WAS OVERRUN BY INFIDELS. SOMETHING HAD TO BE DONE. WHEN THE POPE CALLED FOR A CRUSADE, THE RESPONSE WAS ENTHUSIASTIC.

IF THE CRUSADES DID NOT PERMANENTLY SUCCEED IN THEIR HOLY MISSIONS, THEY HAD DRAMATIC AFTER-EFFECTS ON EUROPEAN FEUDAL SOCIETY.

FOR THE CRUSADING KNIGHTS THE WEALTH AND VITALITY OF CITIES LIKE VENICE AND CONSTANTINOPLE MUST HAVE SEEMED UNREAL. HERE, THE WORLD WAS ON DISPLAY IN SHARP CONTRAST TO THE DREARY LIFE THEY HAD LEFT BEHIND.

AS FOR THE PEASANTS BACK HOME - MANY TOOK THE OPPORTUNITY TO ESCAPE THEIR FEUDAL TIES AND MAKE FOR THE TOWNS, WHICH WERE SWELLING WITH MONEY AND TRADE.

THIS RENEWED INTEREST IN TRADE AND MONEY-LENDING BROUGHT ABOUT A STRONG REACTION FROM THE CATHOLIC CHURCH AND ONE MONK IN PARTICULAR.

AQUINAS FOLLOWED CLOSELY THE WRITINGS OF ARISTOTLE CONCERNING **VALUE** AND **USURY**.

AS FOR VALUE, OR AS AQUINAS PUT IT, '**JUST PRICE**,' HIS ARGUMENT WENT SOMETHING LIKE THIS.

WHILE AQUINAS CAST A SUSPICIOUS EYE ON MERCHANTS AND POINTED AN ACCUSATORY FINGER TOWARD PROFITABLE ONES, HE CONDEMNED TO HELL FOR ALL ETERNITY ANYONE WHO COMMITTED USURY.

AGAIN, LIKE ARISTOTLE, AQUINAS SAW MONEY AS BARREN AND THEREFORE NOT IN IT-SELF ABLE TO INCREASE IN VALUE. IF THIS WERE SO, ASKED HIS PEERS, WHAT THEN COULD A MONEY-LENDER RECEIVE FROM HIS MONEY WITHOUT COMMITTING A MORTAL SIN?

NEVER MIND THAT THE CATHOLIC CHURCH LOANED HUGE SUMS AT HIGH INTEREST RATES... WHAT AQUINAS HAD TO SAY BECAME CANON AND THE CHURCH WAS THE HIGHEST AUTHORITY.

AND SO IT FOLLOWED THAT IN A PREDOMINANTLY CATHOLIC EUROPE THOSE WHO BECAME BANKERS AND MERCHANTS WERE OFTEN JEWISH OR PERHAPS PROTESTANT BEFORE THEIR TIME.

MOVING ON QUICKLY NOW

ABOUT 1300 THE CRUSADERS THREW IN THE TOWEL FOR GOOD AND WENT HOME. UNFORTUNATELY, THEY WEREN'T ALWAYS WELCOME. PEASANTS WERE UNRULY AND UP-START MERCHANTS WANTED CASH.

WORSE YET, GUNPOWDER MADE ITS WAY INTO EUROPE AND CASTLE WALLS WERE COMING DOWN.

FEUDAL KNIGHTS ALLIED AND EMERGED AS SOLIDIFIED NATIONS. WITHOUT CRUSADERS TO DEFEND THE 'HOLY LANDS,' TURKS AND MONGOLS RAN AMOK. TRADE ROUTES TO THE FAR EAST WERE SOON CUT OFF. IF ONLY A NEW TRADE ROUTE COULD BE FOUND.... ON THE RELIGIOUS FRONT **MARTIN LUTHER** ASKED THE QUESTION, "WHAT IF ROME ISN'T THE CENTER OF THE UNIVERSE AFTER ALL?" AN ASTRONOMER TURNED NAVIGATOR, **CHRISTOPHER COLUMBUS**, SUGGESTED THAT THE WORLD WAS ROUND. IF SO, REASONED SPAIN, THEN THEIR BACK-DOOR COUNTRY COULD BECOME A FRONT DOOR TO THE RICHES OF THE FAR EAST.

AND IF NOT? OH WELL, THE GUY **WAS** ITALIAN, AND BESIDES, EVERYONE'S CURIOSITY HAD TO BE SATISFIED SOMETIME...

TO EVERYONE'S SURPRISE COLUMBUS DID RETURN, AND HE BROUGHT BACK NEWS OF A NEW WORLD AND A COUPLE OF HEATHENS EAGER TO CONVERT TO CATHOLICISM. A GRATEFUL POPE GRANTED SPAIN DEED TO MUCH OF THE NEW WORLD...
FIRST THING YOU LEARN IS TO KNEEL
... A NOT SO GRATEFUL HENRY VIII WITH SOUR NUPTIALS TO BOOT SENT THE ROMAN CATHOLICS PACKING...
G'WAN GET OUTTA' HERE, MR. POPE.
ACROSS THE CHANNEL A GUY NAMED JOHN CALVIN INSPIRED THE PROTESTANT FAITH WHEN HE PROPOSED THAT IT WAS O.K. TO MAKE ALOT OF MONEY - SO LONG AS YOU WORKED REAL HARD TO GET IT.
IT SEEMED CALVIN'S TIMING COULDN'T HAVE BEEN BETTER SINCE IT WAS SOON REVEALED THAT THE NEW WORLD HAD GOLD AND SILVER... AND LOTS OF IT.
SURE GOD WANTS US TO MAKE LOTS OF MONEY. JUST DON'T GO SPENDING IT!
NATURALLY THIS PLEASED THE SPANISH MOST SINCE THEY WERE THE FIRST IN LINE. AND, JUST AS XENOPHON, THE GREEK, THEORIZED, SPAIN PROSPERED... BUT AS THE SILVER CONTINUED TO FLOW AND FLOW AND FLOW PRICES IN SPAIN WENT UP AND UP AND UP... UNTIL THE INCREASE IN PRICES NEARLY EQUALED THE INCREASE IN GOLD AND SILVER. WHY DID THIS HAPPEN?
BECAUSE SPAIN HAD ONLY INCREASED THE SUPPLY OF MONEY IN HER COUNTRY AND NOTHING ELSE.
WORLD

WHICH BRINGS US TO...

THE QUANTITY THEORY of MONEY

A FRENCH LAWYER, JEAN BODIN, OBSERVED THAT, "PRICES GO UP OR DOWN DEPENDING DIRECTLY ON THE AMOUNT OF MONEY IN CIRCULATION." THOUGH IT WOULD BE REFINED IN LATER YEARS IT WAS A SIMPLE YET ACCURATE OBSERVATION OF THE DAY.

BUT ALL OTHER THINGS DON'T REMAIN EQUAL FOR LONG. IN SEARCH OF LOWER PRICED GOODS, SPANISH SILVER FLOWED NORTH INTO THE REST OF EUROPE. THIS CAUSED MONEY TO SUDDENLY BECOME A PRINCIPAL PART OF ALMOST EVERYONE'S LIFE. EVEN SERFS WHO FOR CENTURIES HAD PAID THEIR TAXES IN GRAIN AND DAYS' LABOR WERE NOW EXPECTED TO PAY IN CASH.

BANKING COMES TO EUROPE

AS PEOPLE ACCUMULATED MORE MONEY THEY FOUND THEY NEEDED A SAFE PLACE IN WHICH TO STORE IT. GOLDSMITHS WERE GENERALLY ELECTED FOR THE JOB SINCE THEY HAD THE BEST LOCKBOXES IN TOWN. AS SUCH, GOLDSMITHS BECAME EUROPES FIRST BANKERS AND THUS DISCOVERED SOMETHING WONDERFUL...

BOB FOUND THAT HIS PAPER RECEIPT WAS AS GOOD AS HIS SILVER. PEOPLE ACCEPTED IT FOR PAYMENT BECAUSE THEY KNEW THAT AT ANY TIME THEY COULD TAKE IT BACK TO JIM FOR THE ORIGINAL SILVER. KNOWING THIS, PEOPLE CIRCULATED THE PAPER RECEIPTS AS MONEY (GOOD AS GOLD) AND AS SUCH THESE RECEIPTS MIGHT NEVER RETURN TO WHOEVER ISSUED THEM.

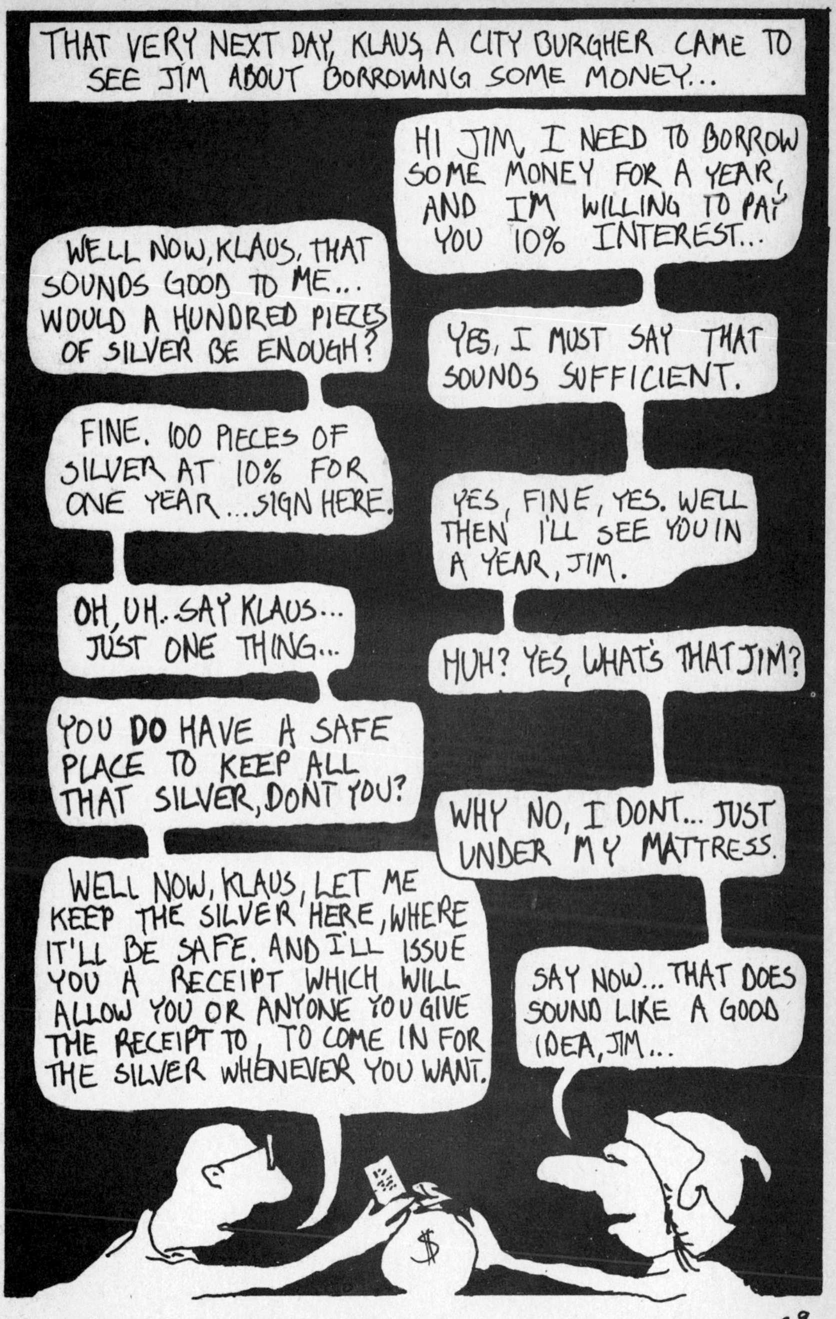
THAT VERY NEXT DAY, KLAUS, A CITY BURGHER CAME TO SEE JIM ABOUT BORROWING SOME MONEY...
HI JIM, I NEED TO BORROW SOME MONEY FOR A YEAR, AND I'M WILLING TO PAY YOU 10% INTEREST...
WELL NOW, KLAUS, THAT SOUNDS GOOD TO ME... WOULD A HUNDRED PIECES OF SILVER BE ENOUGH?
YES, I MUST SAY THAT SOUNDS SUFFICIENT.
FINE. 100 PIECES OF SILVER AT 10% FOR ONE YEAR ...SIGN HERE.
YES, FINE, YES. WELL THEN I'LL SEE YOU IN A YEAR, JIM.
OH, UH.. SAY KLAUS... JUST ONE THING...
HUH? YES, WHAT'S THAT JIM?
YOU **DO** HAVE A SAFE PLACE TO KEEP ALL THAT SILVER, DONT YOU?
WHY NO, I DONT... JUST UNDER MY MATTRESS.
WELL NOW, KLAUS, LET ME KEEP THE SILVER HERE, WHERE IT'LL BE SAFE. AND I'LL ISSUE YOU A RECEIPT WHICH WILL ALLOW YOU OR ANYONE YOU GIVE THE RECEIPT TO, TO COME IN FOR THE SILVER WHENEVER YOU WANT.
SAY NOW... THAT DOES SOUND LIKE A GOOD IDEA, JIM...
$

HOW JIM CAN CREATE MONEY
ORIGINAL BAG OF 100 PIECES OF SILVER HELD BY JIM FOR BOB.
JIM ISSUES NOTE TO BOB VERIFYING THE DEPOSIT OF 100 PIECES OF SILVER.
BOB USES THAT NOTE TO PAY HIS RENT. THE NOTE CIRCULATES BECOMING MONEY.
JIM LOANS THE ORIGINAL BAG OF SILVER TO KLAUS, THEN PERSUADES KLAUS TO DEPOSIT THE SILVER BACK WITH HIM FOR SAFEKEEPING.
JIM ISSUES KLAUS A NOTE TO VERIFY HIS DEPOSIT OF SILVER. KLAUS THEN USES THAT NOTE TO PURCHASE GOODS. THAT NOTE IS NOW MONEY.
ORIGINAL DEPOSIT OF ACTUAL SILVER... 100
BOB'S NOTE OF DEPOSIT... 100
KLAUS' NOTE OF DEPOSIT .. 100
NEW MONEY SUPPLY 300
NOT TO MENTION THE 10 PIECES OF SILVER JIM WILL RECEIVE FROM KLAUS AS INTEREST ON HIS LOAN, INTEREST ON MONEY JIM CREATED.
MOVE OVER ARISTOTLE. FORGET ST. THOMAS.
MODERN BANKING HAD ARRIVED TO CHANGE THE CHARACTER AND PACE OF EUROPEAN LIFE FOR GOOD.

Q: SO WHAT'S TO KEEP JIM FROM WRITING UP ANY NUMBER OF NOTES OF DEPOSIT (ALSO KNOWN AS SILVER CERTIFICATES) AND CIRCULATING THOSE NOTES AS MONEY..?

WE'LL ASK JIM ~

INDEED, SO LONG AS PEOPLE BELIEVED THAT JIM'S NOTES WERE GOOD, HIS SILVER CERTIFICATES CIRCULATED AS MONEY. BUT AS SOON AS DOUBT SET IN...
"THIS GUY JIM GOOD FOR IT?"
"OH HEY, THE GUY IS A SAINT."
I DON'T KNOW THIS GUY JIM,.. I WANT MY SILVER.
WHY SHOULD THEY GET THEIR SILVER BEFORE I GET MINE..?
MAYBE I BETTER GET OVER TO JIM'S JUST IN CASE.
JIM'S
OPEN UP
OPEN UP
YA DEVIL
UH OH
...PEOPLE RUSHED TO CONVERT THEIR PAPER TO METAL. IF A SUFFICIENT AMOUNT OF METAL WAS ON HAND, PANIC COULD BE AVERTED. IF NOT..? WELL THE MESSY SCENE WOULD BE REPEATED TIME AND AGAIN THROUGHOUT HISTORY.

THE MOST NOTABLE BANK FAILURE OF THIS SORT OCCURRED IN FRANCE AND IS WORTH RETELLING HERE. WHEN LOUIS XIV DIED HE LEFT FRANCE DEEPLY IN DEBT. HIS REGENT, THE DUC d'ORLEANS, WAS CONSIDERED NEITHER COMPETENT NOR SCRUPULOUS, ONLY DESPERATE AND GREATLY SO.

JOHN LAW, A SCOTSMAN WHOSE FATHER WAS A GOLDSMITH TURNED BANKER, WAS WELL ACQUAINTED WITH HOW EASILY MONEY COULD BE CREATED. INDEED, HIS PROPOSAL TO THE REGENT WAS SEDUCTIVELY SIMPLE.

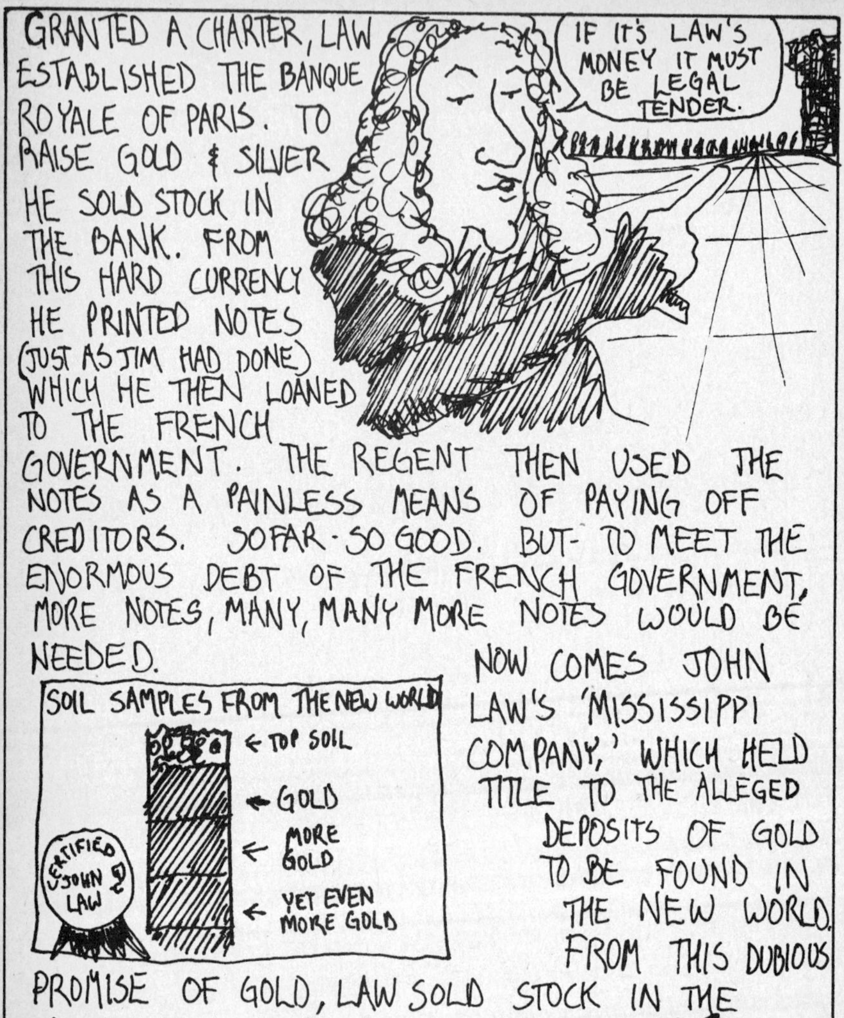
GRANTED A CHARTER, LAW ESTABLISHED THE BANQUE ROYALE OF PARIS. TO RAISE GOLD & SILVER HE SOLD STOCK IN THE BANK. FROM THIS HARD CURRENCY HE PRINTED NOTES (JUST AS JIM HAD DONE) WHICH HE THEN LOANED TO THE FRENCH GOVERNMENT. THE REGENT THEN USED THE NOTES AS A PAINLESS MEANS OF PAYING OFF CREDITORS. SOFAR-SO GOOD. BUT- TO MEET THE ENORMOUS DEBT OF THE FRENCH GOVERNMENT, MORE NOTES, MANY, MANY MORE NOTES WOULD BE NEEDED.
IF IT'S LAW'S MONEY IT MUST BE LEGAL TENDER.
SOIL SAMPLES FROM THE NEW WORLD
TOP SOIL
GOLD
MORE GOLD
YET EVEN MORE GOLD
CERTIFIED BY JOHN LAW
NOW COMES JOHN LAW'S 'MISSISSIPPI COMPANY,' WHICH HELD TITLE TO THE ALLEGED DEPOSITS OF GOLD TO BE FOUND IN THE NEW WORLD. FROM THIS DUBIOUS PROMISE OF GOLD, LAW SOLD STOCK IN THE MISSISSIPPI COMPANY. BIDDING WAS FURIOUS, PRICES WENT UP BY THE HOUR. SO PROSPEROUS WERE SOME FRENCHMEN THAT A NEW TERM WAS COINED TO DESCRIBE THEIR WEALTH
I'M A... A... A... MILLIONAIRE!

BUT! MONEY RAISED BY THE SALE OF STOCK NEVER WENT TO DIG FICTITIOUS GOLD IN LOUISIANA. THE MONEY WENT RIGHT BACK TO JOHN LAW AND THE REGENT. WHERE IT COULD FINANCE EVEN MORE GOVT. SPENDING.
TO SIMPLIFY...
BANK ROYALE
GO
GO
PRINTED MONEY WHICH WAS LOANED TO THE FRENCH GOVT.
100 SHARES MISSISSIPPI CO.
BACK AGAIN TO THE GOVT.
RATTLE RATTLE
LOUIS XV
USED LAW'S PRINTED MONEY TO PAY BACK THE MANY CREDITORS OF THE FRENCH CROWN
NEWLY PAID CREDITORS INVESTED MONEY IN THE MISSISSIPPI CO.

WITH EACH CYCLE, THE FLOOD OF WORTHLESS MONEY CHASING WORTHLESS STOCKS INCREASED UNTIL FINALLY THE FEVER REACHED SUCH A PITCH THAT DOUBT SET IN. AS HAD HAPPENED TO JIM - FRENCHMEN STORMED LAW'S BANK IN HOPES OF REDEEMING THEIR PAPER FOR GOLD. SO GREAT WAS THE CRUSH THAT 15 PEOPLE DIED. NEEDLESS TO SAY - LAW'S BANK FAILED...

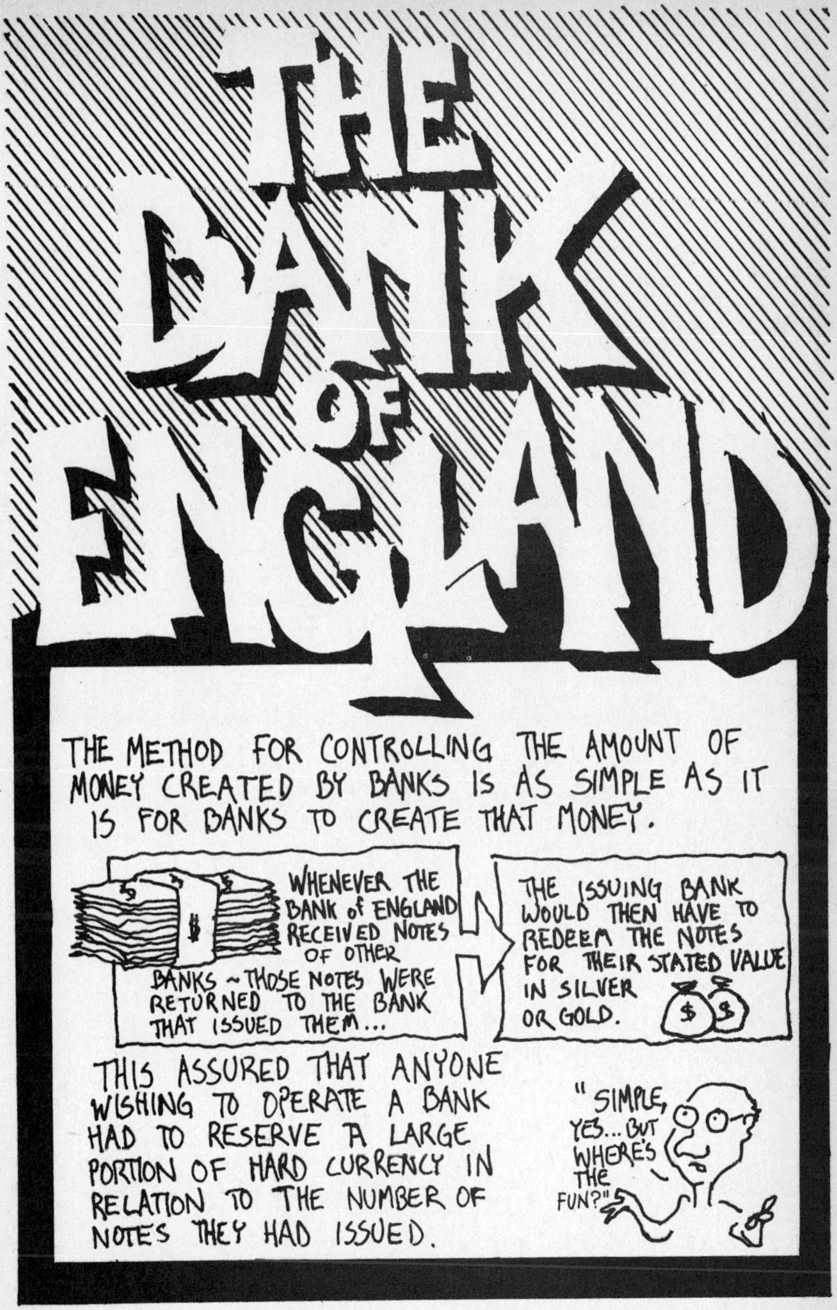
THE BANK OF ENGLAND
THE METHOD FOR CONTROLLING THE AMOUNT OF MONEY CREATED BY BANKS IS AS SIMPLE AS IT IS FOR BANKS TO CREATE THAT MONEY.
WHENEVER THE BANK of ENGLAND RECEIVED NOTES OF OTHER BANKS ~ THOSE NOTES WERE RETURNED TO THE BANK THAT ISSUED THEM...
THE ISSUING BANK WOULD THEN HAVE TO REDEEM THE NOTES FOR THEIR STATED VALUE IN SILVER OR GOLD.
THIS ASSURED THAT ANYONE WISHING TO OPERATE A BANK HAD TO RESERVE A LARGE PORTION OF HARD CURRENCY IN RELATION TO THE NUMBER OF NOTES THEY HAD ISSUED.
"SIMPLE, YES... BUT WHERE'S THE FUN?"

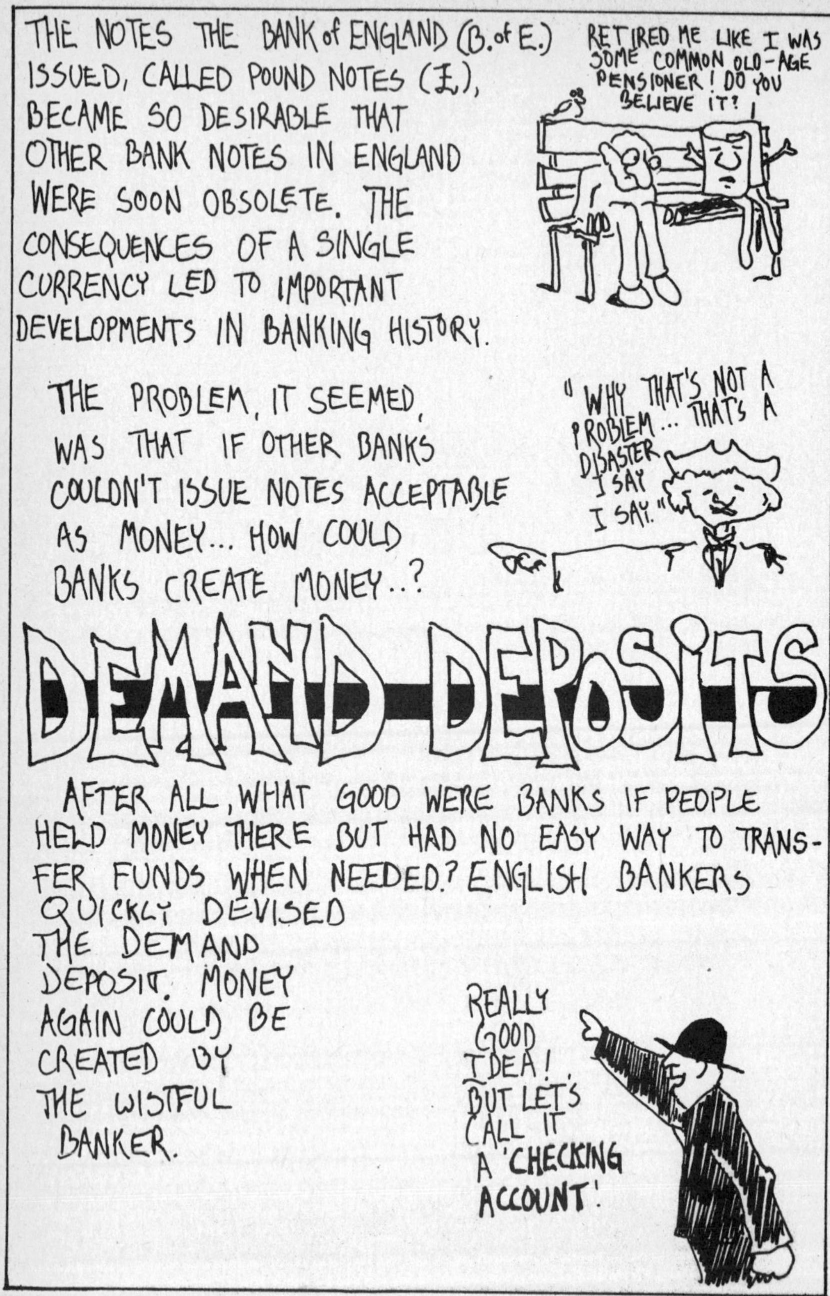
THE NOTES THE BANK of ENGLAND (B. of E.) ISSUED, CALLED POUND NOTES (£), BECAME SO DESIRABLE THAT OTHER BANK NOTES IN ENGLAND WERE SOON OBSOLETE. THE CONSEQUENCES OF A SINGLE CURRENCY LED TO IMPORTANT DEVELOPMENTS IN BANKING HISTORY.
RETIRED ME LIKE I WAS SOME COMMON OLD-AGE PENSIONER! DO YOU BELIEVE IT?
THE PROBLEM, IT SEEMED, WAS THAT IF OTHER BANKS COULDN'T ISSUE NOTES ACCEPTABLE AS MONEY... HOW COULD BANKS CREATE MONEY...?
"WHY THAT'S NOT A PROBLEM... THAT'S A DISASTER I SAY I SAY."
DEMAND DEPOSITS
AFTER ALL, WHAT GOOD WERE BANKS IF PEOPLE HELD MONEY THERE BUT HAD NO EASY WAY TO TRANSFER FUNDS WHEN NEEDED? ENGLISH BANKERS QUICKLY DEVISED THE DEMAND DEPOSIT. MONEY AGAIN COULD BE CREATED BY THE WISTFUL BANKER.
REALLY GOOD IDEA! BUT LET'S CALL IT A 'CHECKING ACCOUNT'.

FINE TUNING

PERHAPS THE MOST IMPORTANT DISCOVERY OF THE DIRECTORS OF THE BANK of ENGLAND WAS THE SIMPLE WAY THEY COULD CONTROL THE AMOUNT OF MONEY IN CIRCULATION. AND THIS IN TURN WOULD AFFECT THE LEVEL OF PRICES (THE QUANTITY THEORY OF MONEY), WHICH WOULD ULTIMATELY AFFECT THE OVERALL LEVEL OF ECONOMIC ACTIVITY (UP or DOWN).

HERE'S HOW...

FOR EXAMPLE:

THE TOWER BANK of PICCADILLY CIRCUS WANTS TO OPEN NEW ACCOUNTS FOR CUSTOMERS WHO WILL BORROW MONEY FROM THE BANK. THE BANK WILL ISSUE CHECKS WHICH CAN BE DRAFTED AGAINST THE ACCOUNT AND DISBURSED IN POUNDS STERLING. TO DO THIS THE BANK MUST INCREASE ITS RESERVE OF (£) NOTES.

TO INCREASE THIS RESERVE THE TOWER BANK BORROWS (£'s) DIRECTLY FROM THE B. of E. SHOULD THE BANK of ENGLAND WANT TO SEE THE MONEY SUPPLY EXPAND IT WOULD SET A LOW **BANK RATE.** (→) CONVERSELY, A HIGH BANK RATE WOULD SHRINK THE CREATION OF NEW MONEY AND BRING PRICES DOWN.

BANK RATE

KNOWN IN U.S. AS THE DISCOUNT RATE

THE RATE OF INTEREST BANKS PAY TO BORROW MONEY FROM A CENTRAL BANK.

CLEARLY BY THE MID 1700's BANKING WAS AHEAD OF ITS TIME. 18th CENTURY EUROPE WAS STILL A LARGELY FEUDAL SOCIETY. MOST EUROPEANS WERE STILL RURAL PEASANTS TIED TO TINY PLOTS OF LAND AND SUBSERVIENT TO THE LOCAL NOBILITY.

BUT THINGS WERE NOT ALWAYS SO GREAT IN THE TOWNS AND CITIES. THE LITTLE BIT OF MANUFACTURING BEING DONE WAS TIGHTLY CONTROLLED BY **GUILDS** ~ SMALL BUT POWERFUL GROUPS THAT DISCOURAGED INNOVATION AND RESTRICTED ENTRY.

BUT THE TIES OF TRADITION AND GUILD CONTROL WERE QUICKLY COMING UNDONE.

ODDLY, THE TRANSFORMATION OF WESTERN SOCIETY FROM AGRARIAN TO INDUSTRIAL WAS DUE IN SOME PART TO SHEEP. AS THE MARKET FOR WOOLENS PICKED UP (FIRST IN BRITAIN), LANDED NOBILITY FOUND THAT THEY COULD DO BETTER FOR THEMSELVES IF THEY USED THE LAND FOR RAISING SHEEP RATHER THAN CONTINUE THEIR CENTURIES-OLD RELATIONSHIP WITH TENANT SERFS.

THE ENCLOSURE ACTS

(OR THE CLEARANCES)...CAUSED THE DISPLACEMENT OF THOUSANDS OF SERFS. THESE PEASANTS WERE FORCED OFF LAND THAT HAD BEEN COMMUNAL FOR CENTURIES BUT WAS NOW BEING CLAIMED BY NOBILITY.

1. IF ANY PEASANT DOUBTED THE NOTION OF PRIVATE OWNERSHIP OF LAND BEFORE, HE DIDN'T NOW. LAND WAS OWNED. OWNERS HAD RIGHTS. AND AS FOR PEASANTS· THEY JUST HAD TO MOVE ON.

2. DISPLACED PEASANTS HAD NOTHING NOW. NO TIES, NO TRADITION, NO PROPERTY, ONLY THE NEED FOR WAGES. THIS WAS THE BEGINNING OF LABOR.

REVIEW
COMMAND, TRADITION OR MARKET... I TELL YOU I DON'T CARE SO LONG AS I CAN STEER CLEAR OF ECONOMISTS!
SO FAR WE'VE SHOWN HOW FROM THE BEGINNING MAN SOUGHT TO ORGANIZE HIMSELF INTO A COMMUNITY SO THAT HE, WITH OTHERS, COULD LIVE SAFELY AND PROSPER.
NOW WHAT? I MEAN WHO DOES WHAT?
SIMPLE. I'LL BE KING AND I'LL DECIDE WHO DOES WHAT.
AS PEOPLE BANDED TOGETHER SOME IMMEDIATE PROBLEMS AROSE. HOW WOULD THINGS GET DONE? WHO WOULD DECIDE WHO DID WHAT? AND FINALLY, WHO WOULD GET HOW MUCH?

WE ALSO KNOW THAT PEOPLE SOLVED THESE PROBLEMS IN ONE OF THREE BASIC WAYS. THE COMMAND ECONOMY, THE TRADITION AND THE MARKET.
THE COMMAND
WHAT! THE SALT MINES! BUT MY DOCTOR SAYS I GOTTA' STAY AWAY FROM SODIUM.
PEOPLE DID THINGS IN A COMMAND ECONOMY BECAUSE NOT DOING THEM MEANT THAT THEY WOULD DIE OR BE SENT SOME PLACE UNPLEASANT.
THE TRADITION
GOSH DAD! YOU MEAN IT! I GET TO WEAR YOUR SHACKLES! —
YOU DID THINGS BECAUSE YOUR PARENTS DID THEM BECAUSE THEIR PARENTS DID THEM AND SO ON AND SO ON...
& THE MARKET
APPLE FOR AN ORANGE
A DEAL
HERE PEOPLE SIMPLY TRADED WHAT THEY HAD FOR WHAT THEY WANTED.

IN FACT, ALL SOCIETIES EXHIBIT A MIXTURE OF ALL THREE ECONOMIC STRUCTURES. HOWEVER, THROUGH HISTORY COMMAND AND TRADITION SEEM TO BE THE ODDS-ON FAVORITES, WITH THE MARKET ECONOMY TAKING A SORT OF BACK-SEAT, SATURDAY AFTERNOON POSITION.

TOO BAD, SINCE THE MARKET ECONOMY SEEMS THE MOST EQUITABLE OF THE THREE. BUT AS WE'VE SHOWN, FOR THE MARKET ECONOMY TO DOMINATE PEOPLE HAVE TO DEVELOP AND ACCEPT A FEW THINGS. THINGS LIKE MONEY, BANKING, PRIVATE PROPERTY, LABOR AND, OF COURSE, THE PROFIT-MOTIVATED ENTREPRENEUR.

FINALLY, BEFORE WE MOVE ON TO PART 2 IT IS WORTH NOTING THAT SOME OF THE MORE IMPORTANT EVENTS IN HISTORY WITH ECONOMIC CONSEQUENCES WERE NOT THE RESULT OF CAREFUL PLANNING AND DELIBERATION TO SEEK A BETTER WORLD FOR THE COMMON MAN. NEARLY ALL WERE STUMBLED UPON BY SIMPLE ACCIDENT. CHRISTOPHER COLUMBUS DIDN'T SET OUT TO FIND A NEW WORLD TO GIVE HOPE TO EUROPE'S MANY OPPRESSED PEASANTS. COLUMBUS MERELY SOUGHT A QUICKER TRADE ROUTE WEST TO INDIA & CHINA. WHEN THE SPANISH DISCOVERED HUGE DEPOSITS OF GOLD AND SILVER IN THE NEW WORLD THEY WERE PLEASED, NOT BECAUSE IT WOULD REVOLUTIONIZE EUROPE'S MEDIEVAL ATTITUDE ABOUT MONEY, BUT BECAUSE THE GOLD WOULD ENRICH THEM AND THE SPANISH REALM. AND FINALLY IT WAS THE PROFITABLE WOOL OF SHEEP WHICH ENDED THE CENTURIES-OLD TIES BETWEEN NOBILITY AND SERFS AND BROUGHT ABOUT TWO IMPORTANT FEATURES OF THE MARKET SOCIETY, LAND AND LABOR.

PART 2
THE OPEN MARKET
COMMAND
TRADITION
OPEN MARKET

THE OPEN MARKET SOCIETY WAS LIKE A GIANT TRADING TABLE WHERE EVERY MEMBER CAME AS A BUYER OR SELLER OR BOTH. NOT ONLY WERE FINISHED GOODS BEING TRADED, THE **OPEN MARKET** MADE AVAILABLE THE **MEANS** TO PRODUCE **FUTURE** GOODS... KNOWN AS **'THE FACTORS OF PRODUCTION'**.

NOTE: WHILE WE'VE BEEN CAREFUL TO NOTE THE IMPORTANCE OF MONEY AND BANKING AND CHANGES IN ATTITUDES AND SOCIAL STRUCTURES WHICH PAVED THE WAY TO AN OPEN MARKET SOCIETY, NONE OF THIS COULD HAVE HAPPENED HAD A LEGAL SYSTEM NOT DEVELOPED WHICH RECOGNIZED PROPERTY, CONTRACTS AND INDIVIDUAL RIGHTS.

THE FACTORS of PRODUCTION

LAND 

LABOR 

CAPITAL 

AND THE ENTREPRENEUR 

AS WE'VE MENTIONED, THE OPEN MARKET MAKES AVAILABLE THE **FACTORS OF PRODUCTION** (ALL OF WHICH ARE COMMODITIES: LAND WHICH MAY BE RENTED, LABOR HIRED AND MONEY BORROWED) TO THE ENTREPRENEUR...

INDEED THE ENTREPRENEUR HAS JUST ONE SPECIAL QUALIFICATION... JUST ONE.

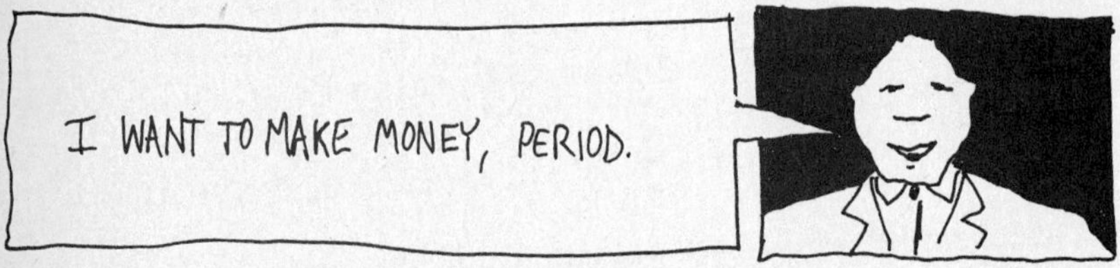

NO DOUBT. THE ENTREPRENEUR IS MOTIVATED BY **PROFIT**. NO MATTER HOW PERSONALLY VILE OR SAINTLY THE ENTREPRENEUR MAY BE, HIS SINGLE AIM IS THE GREATER ACCUMULATION OF MONEY!

AND SO IT WAS FOR ENGLISH SOCIETY DURING THE LATTER 1700'S, WHERE THE OPEN MARKET ECONOMY WAS ABOUT TO EMERGE. IN FACT, ALL THAT WAS NEEDED WAS FOR SOMEONE TO COME ALONG AND EXPLAIN IT ALL.

1776. ADAM SMITH PUBLISHED HIS BOOK, "**THE WEALTH of NATIONS.**" THE BOOK DETAILED THE WORKINGS AND FUTURE POSSIBILITIES OF THE OPEN MARKET. IN IT HE SAW A SOCIETY WHERE ALL PARTICIPANTS INCLUDING THE ENTREPRENEUR ARE GUIDED BY SELF-INTEREST (OR AN '**INVISIBLE HAND**' AS SMITH PUTS IT) IN THE DIRECTION WHICH IS MOST AGREEABLE TO THE INTEREST OF THE WHOLE SOCIETY.

SINCE THE OPEN MARKET POSED NO MORAL RESTRAINT ON PRICES (SEE: St. THOMAS AQUINAS), EXCESS ON THE PART OF ONE INDIVIDUAL WOULD BE KEPT IN CHECK BY **COMPETITION** FROM OTHER 'LIKE-MINDED' INDIVIDUALS.

THUS COMPETITION SERVED TO BRING PRICES DOWN. SMITH OBSERVED THAT WHEN **PROFITS** (REVENUE LESS COSTS) SHRANK TOO LOW, THE **INVISIBLE HAND** OF SELF-INTEREST SENT SOME COMPETITORS INTO NEW MARKETS WHERE HIGHER PROFITS MIGHT BE FOUND. THIS, IN TURN, ASSURED SOCIETY THAT **LIMITED FACTORS of PRODUCTION** ALWAYS SHIFTED TOWARD PRODUCTS AND SERVICES WHICH PEOPLE WANTED AND NEEDED THE MOST, EVEN AS THOSE NEEDS AND WANTS CHANGED.

TO SMITH, SELF-INTEREST AND COMPETITION WERE TWO COUNTERBALANCING WEIGHTS WHICH COMPELLED EVERYONE IN THE MARKET TOWARD EVENTUAL ENDS THAT WERE SOCIALLY BENEFICIAL. WHILE MARKET FORCES WERE STRONG AND UNIVERSAL, SMITH ALSO RECOGNIZED AN INHERENT WEAKNESS. AS HE PUT IT...
PEOPLE OF THE SAME TRADE SELDOM MEET TOGETHER EVEN FOR MERRIMENT AND DIVERSION, BUT THE CONVERSATION ENDS IN A CONSPIRACY AGAINST THE PUBLIC OR IN SOME CONTRIVANCE TO RAISE PRICES.
WELCOME MANUFACTURERS 1ST ANNUAL SHIN-DIG 1776
NO MORE COMPETITION
CARTEL... CARTEL... CARTEL!
BARRIERS TO ENTRY!
WE'LL KEEP PRICES ARTIFICIALLY HIGH
HERE'S TO FIXED PRICES
HERE HERE

WHILE EFFORTS TO REDUCE COMPETITION PLAGUE THE MARKET EVEN TODAY (E.G., O.P.E.C.) SUCH JOINT CONSPIRACIES ARE PRONE TO FAILURE (E.G., O.P.E.C. AGAIN).

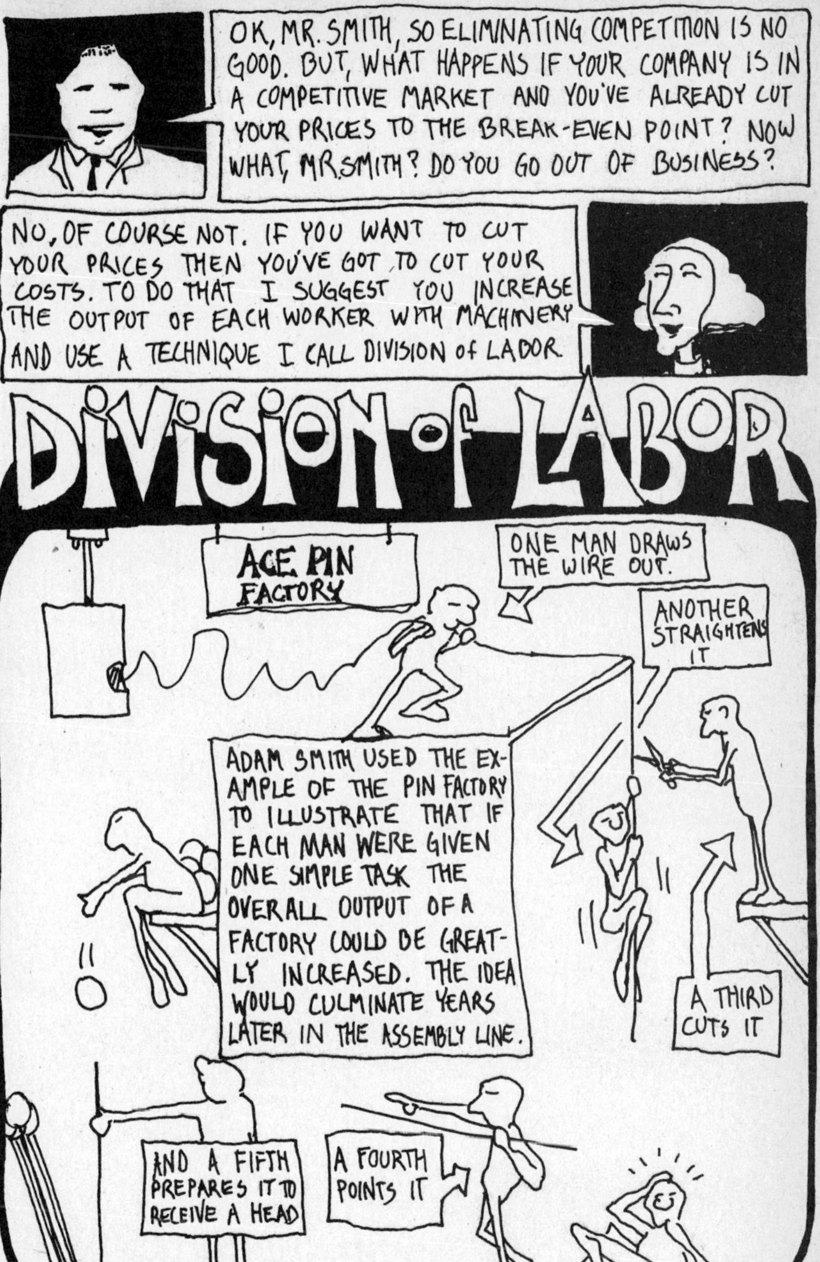
OK, MR. SMITH, SO ELIMINATING COMPETITION IS NO GOOD. BUT, WHAT HAPPENS IF YOUR COMPANY IS IN A COMPETITIVE MARKET AND YOU'VE ALREADY CUT YOUR PRICES TO THE BREAK-EVEN POINT? NOW WHAT, MR. SMITH? DO YOU GO OUT OF BUSINESS?
NO, OF COURSE NOT. IF YOU WANT TO CUT YOUR PRICES THEN YOU'VE GOT TO CUT YOUR COSTS. TO DO THAT I SUGGEST YOU INCREASE THE OUTPUT OF EACH WORKER WITH MACHINERY AND USE A TECHNIQUE I CALL DIVISION OF LABOR
DIVISION OF LABOR
ACE PIN FACTORY
ONE MAN DRAWS THE WIRE OUT.
ANOTHER STRAIGHTENS IT
ADAM SMITH USED THE EXAMPLE OF THE PIN FACTORY TO ILLUSTRATE THAT IF EACH MAN WERE GIVEN ONE SIMPLE TASK THE OVERALL OUTPUT OF A FACTORY COULD BE GREATLY INCREASED. THE IDEA WOULD CULMINATE YEARS LATER IN THE ASSEMBLY LINE.
A THIRD CUTS IT
A FOURTH POINTS IT
AND A FIFTH PREPARES IT TO RECEIVE A HEAD

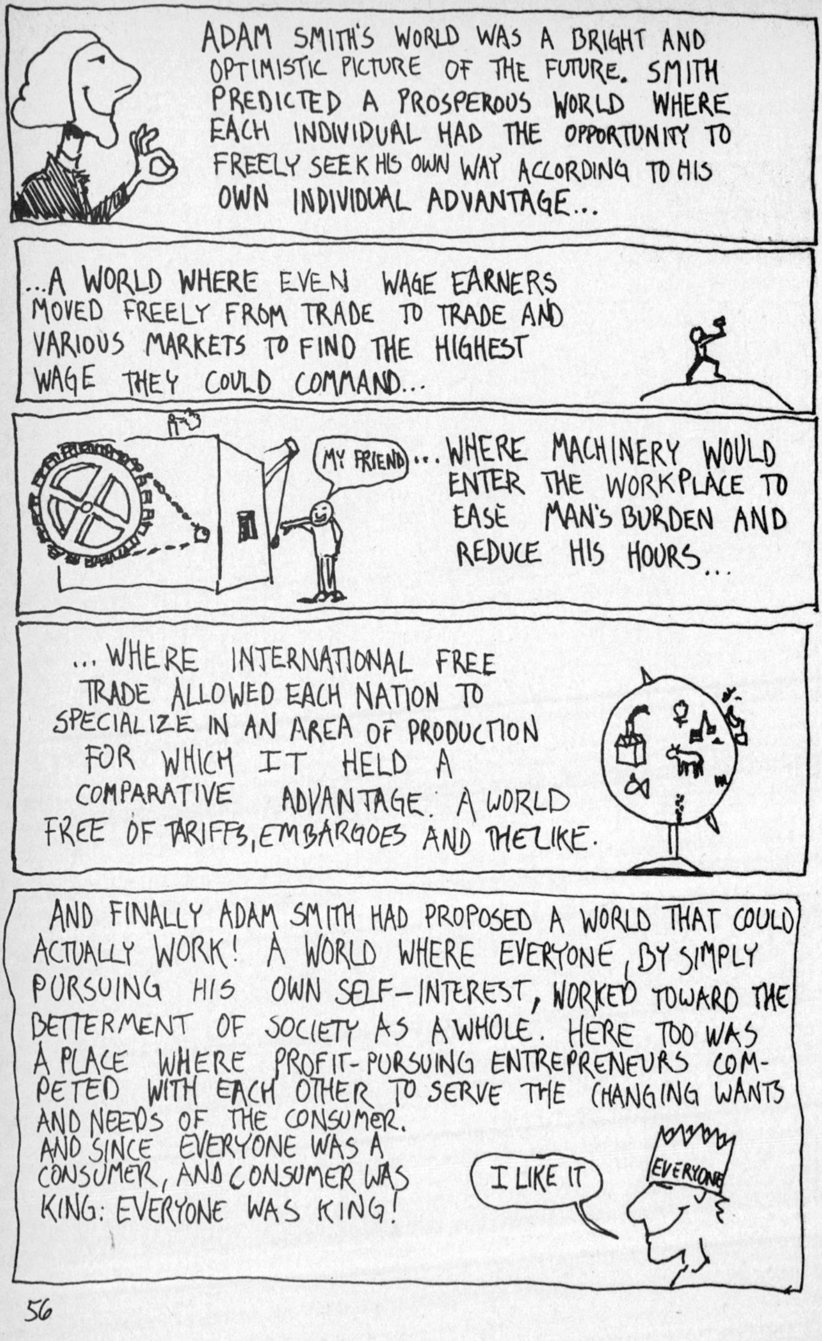
ADAM SMITH'S WORLD WAS A BRIGHT AND OPTIMISTIC PICTURE OF THE FUTURE. SMITH PREDICTED A PROSPEROUS WORLD WHERE EACH INDIVIDUAL HAD THE OPPORTUNITY TO FREELY SEEK HIS OWN WAY ACCORDING TO HIS OWN INDIVIDUAL ADVANTAGE...
...A WORLD WHERE EVEN WAGE EARNERS MOVED FREELY FROM TRADE TO TRADE AND VARIOUS MARKETS TO FIND THE HIGHEST WAGE THEY COULD COMMAND...
MY FRIEND
...WHERE MACHINERY WOULD ENTER THE WORKPLACE TO EASE MAN'S BURDEN AND REDUCE HIS HOURS...
...WHERE INTERNATIONAL FREE TRADE ALLOWED EACH NATION TO SPECIALIZE IN AN AREA OF PRODUCTION FOR WHICH IT HELD A COMPARATIVE ADVANTAGE. A WORLD FREE OF TARIFFS, EMBARGOES AND THE LIKE.
AND FINALLY ADAM SMITH HAD PROPOSED A WORLD THAT COULD ACTUALLY WORK! A WORLD WHERE EVERYONE, BY SIMPLY PURSUING HIS OWN SELF-INTEREST, WORKED TOWARD THE BETTERMENT OF SOCIETY AS A WHOLE. HERE TOO WAS A PLACE WHERE PROFIT-PURSUING ENTREPRENEURS COMPETED WITH EACH OTHER TO SERVE THE CHANGING WANTS AND NEEDS OF THE CONSUMER.
AND SINCE EVERYONE WAS A CONSUMER, AND CONSUMER WAS KING: EVERYONE WAS KING!
I LIKE IT
EVERYONE

SO WHAT WENT WRONG?
FOR ONE THING
ENGLAND INDUSTRIALIZED.
THE RESULT...
ENGLAND'S DISPLACED PEASANTS, HER NEW INDUSTRIAL WORKING CLASS, ENDURED SQUALID CONDITIONS, DANGEROUS MACHINERY, NEARLY ROUND-THE-CLOCK HOURS AND, TO TOP IT OFF, WAGES SO LOW AS TO BE BELOW THE SUBSISTENCE (THE BARE MINIMUM NEEDED FOR SURVIVAL) LEVEL.
YEP... TENDS TO BRING ON A TENSION HEADACHE ALL RIGHT.
MAYBE WE'LL GET TO WORK ON THE SAME LINE
TO SURVIVE, TO JUST SURVIVE, WORKMEN HAD NO CHOICE BUT TO SEND THEIR WIVES AND CHILDREN INTO THE DANGEROUS CONDITIONS OF THE FACTORY.
HEY, NOW WAIT A MINUTE... THIS DIDN'T RESULT FROM THE OPEN MARKET... I NEVER ADVOCATED ANYTHING LIKE THAT!
TRUE ENOUGH... BUT
THEN WHO DID?

REVEREND MALTHUS GAINED QUITE A FOLLOWING IN TURN-OF-THE-CENTURY ENGLAND WITH HIS GLOOMY EQUATIONS THAT SHOWED A RAPIDLY EXPLODING POPULATION RUNNING HEADLONG INTO A FOOD SUPPLY THAT COULD AT BEST INCREASE FRACTIONALLY. MALTHUS' WIDELY ACCEPTED SOLUTION TO THIS COMING DAY OF FAMINE WAS TO STEM THE PROCREATING ABILITY OF ENGLAND'S WORKING CLASS WITH PROLONGED HOURS OF HARSH LABOR FOR AS LITTLE PAY AS POSSIBLE.

TO FURTHER SUBSTANTIATE MALTHUS' BELIEFS CAME DAVID RICARDO. ALTHOUGH THE TWO VARIED ON MOST POINTS, BOTH WERE IN BLEAK AGREEMENT WHEN IT CAME TO THE WORKINGMAN. AS RICARDO SAW IT, WORKERS SHOULD RECEIVE SUBSISTENCE WAGES AND NO MORE. FOR EMPLOYERS TO PAY MORE WAS WASTEFUL, INHUMAN AND POSSIBLY SUBVERSIVE. THIS WAS RICARDO'S IRON-CLAD LAW of WAGES.

THIS IRON-CLAD LAW OF WAGES STEMMED FROM RICARDO'S PERCEPTION OF TOTAL NATIONAL WEALTH AS A PIE THAT ONLY CUT THREE WAYS...

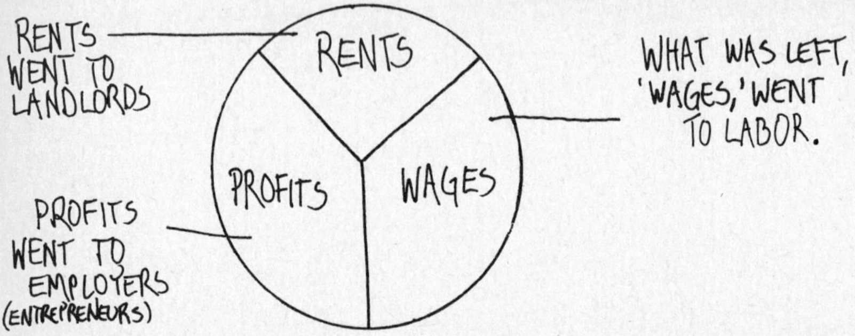

SINCE LAND WAS FIXED IT MEANT THAT AS POPULATION GREW AND CLAIMS FOR LAND INCREASED, RENTS AS A SHARE OF THE PIE HAD TO INCREASE. ALSO, A GROWING POPULATION MEANT A GROWING WORKFORCE WHICH WOULD HAVE TO MEAN A LARGER PIECE OF PIE WOULD GO TO WAGES (EVEN IF INDIVIDUAL WAGE RATES NEVER ROSE).

FALLING PROFITS LEFT EMPLOYERS ONLY ONE RECOURSE; LOWER THE RATE OF WAGES BY BRINGING DOWN THE SUBSISTENCE LEVEL. THIS, RICARDO POINTED OUT, THEY COULD DO WITH A LITTLE HELP FROM THE OPEN MARKET.

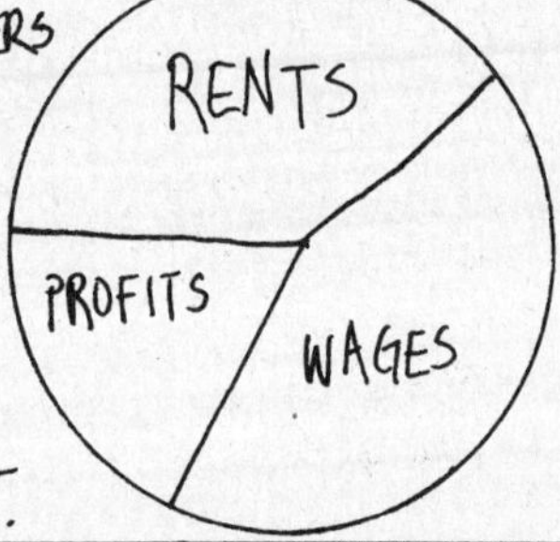

NOTE: DAVID RICARDO'S WRITINGS ARE ONE OF THE MANY INTERESTING PARADOXES OF ECONOMICS. HE WAS, AND STILL IS, KNOWN AS ONE OF ADAM SMITH'S STAUNCHEST DEFENDERS. AND YET IT WAS THE WRITINGS OF RICARDO, MORE THAN ANYONE'S THAT INFLUENCED NONE OTHER THAN KARL MARX, THE OPEN MARKET'S GREATEST CRITIC TO DATE.

RICARDO BELIEVED THAT PRESSURE ON WAGES WAS CONSTANT AND DOWNWARD. AS THE NUMBERS OF WORKERS INCREASED - THEIR COMPETITION FOR JOBS DROVE WAGES DOWN.

WHILE LANDLORDS SOUGHT TO KEEP GRAIN PRICES HIGH (THEIR MAJOR SOURCE OF RENT), ENTREPRENEURIAL INDUSTRIALISTS FOUGHT TO BRING GRAIN PRICES DOWN. SINCE FOR THEM THE PRICE OF GRAIN WAS LINKED DIRECTLY TO THE COST OF WAGES, ANY TIME YOU COULD LOWER GRAIN PRICES YOU COULD LOWER WAGE COSTS.

IN THE WORLD OF MALTHUS AND RICARDO, THERE WAS ONLY ONE HOPE TO IMPROVE THE LOT OF THE WORKING CLASS AND THAT WAS SOMETHING CALLED A POSITIVE CHECK.

AND WHAT WAS A POSITIVE CHECK..?

TO NAME A FEW OF THE POSITIVE CHECKS WHICH SERVED TO THIN THE RANKS OF THE WORKING CLASS: SEVERE WORKING CONDITIONS, SPOILT FOOD, UNSANITARY LIVING QUARTERS, DISEASE, WAR, PLAGUE AND FAMINE.

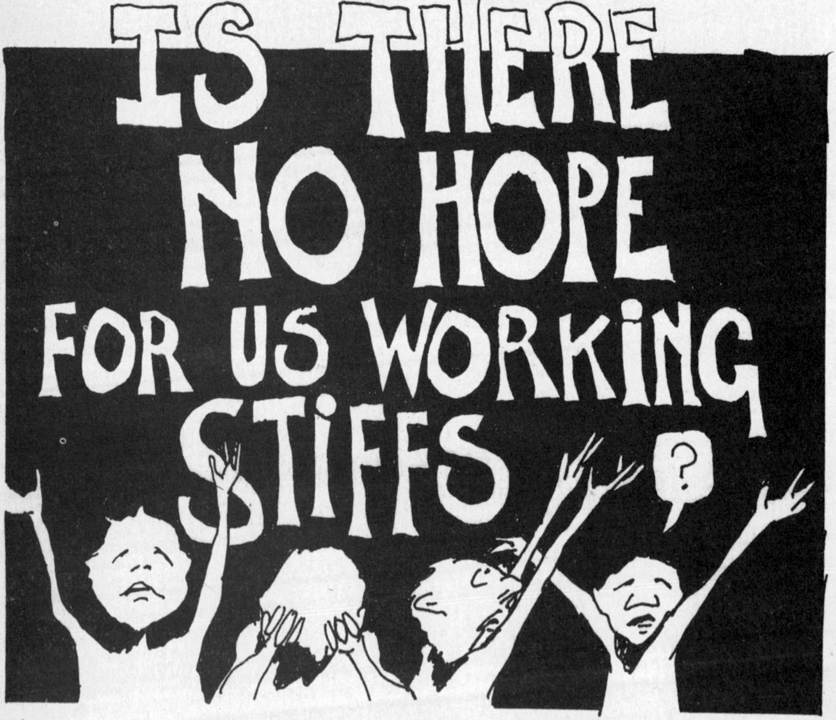

YES, THERE IS! REPEAL THE CORN LAWS WHICH WERE PASSED BY PARLIAMENT TO PROTECT WEALTHY LANDLORD FARMERS FROM THE COMPETITION OF CHEAPER IMPORTED GRAIN. THE CORN LAWS HAVE DONE NOTHING BUT KEEP THE PRICE OF GRAIN (AND THEREIN THE COST OF LIVING) ARTIFICIALLY HIGH.
BUT YOU YOURSELF ADMIT THAT LOWER GRAIN PRICES WILL ONLY RESULT IN EMPLOYERS PAYING LOWER WAGES!
RICARDO
MALTHUS
EVENTUALLY, YES, WAGES WILL FALL. BUT IN THE MEANTIME WORKERS WILL EXPERIENCE SOME MEASURE OF PROSPERITY.
PERHAPS. BUT THEN THEIR NUMBERS WILL INCREASE, CAUSING WAGES TO FALL EVEN LOWER.
MAYBE. MAYBE NOT. WHEN WAGES ARE LOW EMPLOYERS WILL HIRE MORE WORKERS. NEW SHOPS AND FACTORIES WILL OPEN AND EVEN MORE WORKERS WILL BE HIRED..
...THEN IF EXPANSION AND HIRING GROWS AT A FASTER RATE THAN POPULATION - LABOR WILL BECOME SCARCE, AND EMPLOYERS WILL HAVE TO BID UP WAGES, AND THEN WORKERS WILL KNOW REAL PROSPERITY.
BUT WILL EXPANSION AND HIRING EVER EXCEED POPULATION GROWTH? I DONT THINK SO.
HMM... WELL YES, I SUPPOSE YOU'RE RIGHT... TO SAY NOTHING OF THE DWINDLING SUPPLY OF FARMLAND.
OF COURSE! GRAIN PRICES WILL, IN THE END, EXCEED WAGE GAINS.
WELL WE'RE BACK AGAIN TO THE OLD POSITIVE CHECKS.
A GOOD WAR, I THINK.

AS IT TURNED OUT, ENGLAND DID REPEAL THE CORN LAWS. THE RESULT WAS MUCH AS RICARDO HAD PREDICTED (HIS PREDICTIONS WERE DRAWN LARGELY FROM ADAM SMITH'S TEACHINGS).

AS GRAIN PRICES FELL, WORKERS ENJOYED A MODEST INCREASE IN THEIR STANDARD OF LIVING.

AS ENGLAND ENTERED THE LATTER STAGES OF THE INDUSTRIAL PROCESS, REFORMS CAME ABOUT WHICH DECREASED THE AVAILABLE NUMBER OF WORKERS BY RESTRICTING THE HIRING OF WOMEN AND CHILDREN AND LIMITING THE NUMBER OF HOURS IN A WORK DAY. AND CONTRARY TO MALTHUS' PREDICTIONS, THE BIRTH RATE LEVELED OFF. THIS FURTHER LIMITED THE OVERALL LEVEL OF THE AVAILABLE WORKFORCE, RESULTING IN AN UNPRECEDENTED RISE IN THE STANDARD OF LIVING OF THE WORKING CLASS - PARTICULARLY IN COMPARISON TO PRE-INDUSTRIALIZED PEASANTS.

INDUSTRIALIZATION
A LOOK BEHIND THE PROCESS OF INDUSTRIAL CHANGE AND INTO THE THEORY AND DYNAMICS OF HOW IT HAPPENS.

INDUSTRIALIZATION CAN AND DOES RAISE THE MATERIAL WELL-BEING OF A SOCIETY AND ITS MEMBERS.

IN A MARKET SOCIETY THE COMPETITIVE EDGE GOES TO THE PRODUCER (ENTREPRENEUR) WHO CAN OFFER HIS PRODUCT AT THE LOWEST PRICE.

THE INDUSTRIAL PROCESS IS MERELY UTILIZING CAPITAL WHICH HAS BEEN MECHANIZED AND MOTORIZED. AFTER ALL, HORSE-POWER AND ELBOW GREASE COULD ONLY GO SO FAR.

MONEY IN ITSELF IS NOT CAPITAL. HOWEVER, MONEY CAN BE USED TO OBTAIN CAPITAL...

WHAT IS CAPITAL?

CAPITAL CAN BE PRACTICALLY ANYTHING WHICH IS USEFUL TO MAN.

A ROCK, A VINE AND A STICK ARE ALL **CAPITAL** TO A CAVEMAN WHO NEEDS A TOOL. WHEN HE COMBINES THEM HE HAS A TOOL WHICH HE CAN USE TO INCREASE HIS HUNTING (OR PRODUCTIVE) ABILITY.

ECONOMISTS CALL ANY SUCH IMPLEMENT A CAPITAL GOOD.

WHEN A SOCIETY INDUSTRIALIZES: IT PROVIDES WORKERS WITH CAPITAL GOODS (MACHINERY) THAT EMPLOY ADVANCED DEVICES SUCH AS GEARS, HYDRAULICS, STEAM & COMBUSTION WHICH CAN VASTLY ENHANCE MAN'S PRODUCTIVE CAPABILITIES.

ACQUIRING CAPITAL REQUIRES SAVING

THE CAVEMAN WAS IN A CONSTANT SEARCH FOR FOOD. IF HE WANTED TO TAKE THE TIME TO ACQUIRE CAPITAL AND FASHION A CAPITAL GOOD HE HAD TO EITHER PUT ASIDE FOOD OR ABSTAIN FROM EATING. THIS IS TRUE OF ANY SOCIETY, IF ALL MEMBERS ARE ENGAGED IN THE PRODUCTION AND CONSUMPTION OF FOOD, THAT SOCIETY WILL NEVER EXPERIENCE CAPITAL GROWTH. ONLY THROUGH THE PRIOR ACT OF SAVING OR ABSTENTION FROM CONSUMPTION CAN A SOCIETY HOPE TO IMPROVE ITS STORE OF CAPITAL GOODS.

THIS IS DOUBLY TRUE FOR SOCIETIES WISHING TO INDUSTRIALIZE, BECAUSE IN ORDER FOR A SOCIETY TO OBTAIN INDUSTRIAL CAPITAL GOODS WHICH CAN ENHANCE MAN'S PRODUCTIVE CAPACITY (i.e., TRACTORS, COMBINES, ETC.) IT MUST FIRST ACQUIRE RAW INDUSTRIAL CAPITAL (I.E., TECHNOLOGY, FACTORIES, A MEANS OF HARNESSING POWER).

IT OFFERED THE INCENTIVE OF PROFIT WHICH IS FOUND ONLY IN THE OPEN MARKET. IT WAS NO ACCIDENT THAT INDUSTRIALIZATION OCCURRED SHORTLY AFTER THE OPEN MARKET EMERGED IN ENGLAND. COMPETITIVE ENTREPRENEURS SOUGHT PROFITS, CAPITAL GOODS MADE LABOR MORE PRODUCTIVE, MORE PRODUCTIVE LABOR MADE MORE PROFIT, INDUSTRIAL CAPITAL MADE LABOR INFINITELY MORE PRODUCTIVE, INFINITELY MORE PRODUCTIVE LABOR MADE INFINITELY MORE PROFITS.

"AHH, SO THAT'S WHY THEY CALL HIM A 'CAPITALIST.'" –

LABOR. BECAUSE PEOPLE WORKED FOR SUBSISTENCE WAGES CAPITALISTS HAD THAT MUCH MORE MONEY TO RE-INVEST INTO THE CREATION OF GREATER CAPITAL. HAD LABOR BEEN PAID SUBSTANTIALLY MORE, THEIR INCREASED CONSUMPTION WOULD NOT HAVE PERMITTED ENGLAND'S **DRAMATIC** INDUSTRIALIZATION; THE PROCESS WOULD HAVE REQUIRED MUCH MORE TIME.

KARL MARX
A SORT OF 'YOSEMITE SAM OF ECONOMISTS,
KARL WANTED TO TURN THE WHOLE SYSTEM
UPSIDE DOWN - SHAKE IT LOOSE - THROW IT AWAY.

THE INFLUENCES WHICH SHAPED MARX'S THINKING WERE VARIOUS AND MANY. WE DO KNOW, FOR INSTANCE, THAT AS A YOUTH, MARX EXPERIENCED FIRSTHAND THE EFFECTS OF THE ENCLOSURE MOVEMENTS UPON HIS GERMAN BIRTHPLACE. WHAT WERE COMMUNAL FORESTS BECAME, AT ONCE, PRIVATE PROPERTY.

ON TO FRANCE

THROWN OUT OF HIS NATIVE GERMANY FOR EXPRESSING HIS DISTASTE FOR SUCH THINGS AS PRIVATE PROPERTY, MARX MOVED TO PARIS. HERE, DESPITE SOME EARLY DIFFICULTY, MARX PEPPERED HIS VOCABULARY WITH A LITTLE FRENCH.

ON TO BELGIUM

THROWN OUT OF FRANCE, MARX MOVED ON TO BRUSSELS. HERE, WITH HIS LONGTIME FRIEND FRIEDRICH ENGELS, MARX WROTE THE "**COMMUNIST MANIFESTO**," WHICH WAS BOTH A CALL TO ARMS FOR WORKERS TO OVERTHROW THE SYSTEM **AND** AT THE SAME TIME AN ENVIOUS ADMISSION OF CAPITALIST ACHIEVEMENT.

I.E.,

> ... THE BOURGEOISIE HAS CREATED ENORMOUS CITIES, HAS GREATLY INCREASED THE URBAN POPULATION... THUS RESCUING A CONSIDERABLE PART OF THE POPULATION FROM THE IDIOCY OF RURAL LIFE...
>
> ... THE BOURGEOISIE DURING ITS SCANT ONE HUNDRED YEARS, HAS CREATED MORE MASSIVE AND MORE COLOSSAL PRODUCTIVE FORCES THAN HAVE ALL PRECEDING GENERATIONS TOGETHER.

ON TO LONDON

THROWN OUT OF BELGIUM, MARX RETURNED TO FRANCE ONLY TO BE THROWN OUT AGAIN. SO IN 1849 (LESS THAN 75 YEARS SINCE ADAM SMITH PUBLISHED "THE WEALTH OF NATIONS") MARX MOVED TO LONDON AND BEGAN WORK ON HIS MASSIVE HISTORICAL, PHILOSOPHICAL AND ECONOMIC TREATISE,

"DAS KAPITAL"

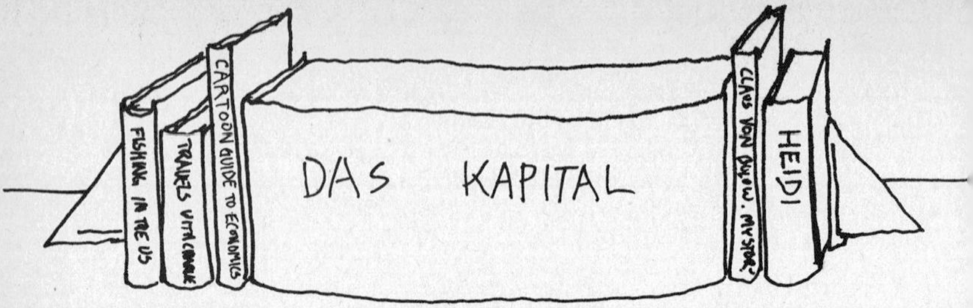

"DAS KAPITAL" RAN A LENGTHY 3000 PAGES, MOST OF WHICH WERE WRITTEN BY ENGELS AFTER MARX'S DEATH.

THEORY of SURPLUS VALUE

ASSUME, AS MARX DID, THAT ALL **WEALTH** IS CREATED BY LABOR. NOW, ASSUME A LABORER WORKS A TWELVE-HOUR DAY (NOT AT ALL UNCOMMON THEN) AND THAT THE LABORER **EARNS** HIS DAY'S WAGE AFTER WORKING ONLY SIX HOURS... THE **VALUE** THAT WORKER CREATES IN THE NEXT SIX HOURS WILL NOT BRING HIM ANY ADDITIONAL PAY BUT RATHER IS EXPROPRIATED BY HIS CAPITALIST EMPLOYER. THEREFORE, ACCORDING TO MARX, **SURPLUS VALUE** IS MERELY THE CAPITALIST'S ABILITY TO OBTAIN WEALTH (THROUGH LABOR) BUT NOT HAVE TO PAY FOR IT.

AND HOW DID HE DO THAT?

FIRST, CUT WAGES, THEN EXTEND THE HOURS IN A WORK DAY. NEXT, HIRE WOMEN AND CHILDREN AND CUT WAGES AGAIN, THEN ADD ANOTHER HOUR OR TWO TO THE WORK DAY.

"WELL," SAID KARL, "YOU COULD BRING IN MACHINERY, **BUT** REMEMBER, ONLY LABOR CREATES VALUE, SO THE ONLY VALUE YOU CAN EXTRACT FROM A MACHINE IS THE VALUE OF LABOR THAT WENT INTO MAKING IT."

RECALL RICARDO'S PIE OF NATIONAL WEALTH . . .

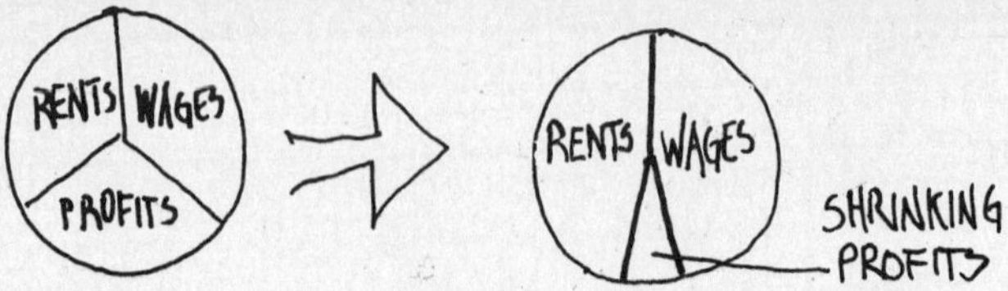

PROFITS SHRANK AS RENTS AND TOTAL WAGE PAYMENTS INCREASED. AS RICARDO SAW IT THERE WAS SIMPLY NO HOPE FOR THE CAPITALIST. IF POPULATION LEVELS FELL, FEWER WORKERS COULD DEMAND HIGHER WAGES. IF POPULATION LEVELS ROSE, RENTS WOULD HAVE TO GO UP.

THE MARXIST PIE

FIRST, MARX ELIMINATED ANY DISTINCTION BETWEEN LANDLORDS AND CAPITALISTS (THE RULING CLASS WAS THE RULING CLASS). THEN HE PREDICTED THAT WORKERS WOULD CURTAIL THEIR BIRTHRATE, REDUCING THE LABOR FORCE, WHICH WOULD THEN PUSH WAGES BACK UP. TO RETALIATE, CAPITALISTS WOULD SEEK TO ADVANCE TECHNOLOGY AT A RAPID PACE. THIS WOULD ACHIEVE TWO GOALS.

1. AS WE KNOW INDUSTRIAL CAPITAL GOODS ENORMOUSLY ENHANCE MAN'S PRODUCTIVE CAPACITY. TO MARX, THIS MEANT A RELATIVE INCREASE IN SURPLUS VALUE SINCE THE NUMBER OF HOURS IN A WORKDAY THAT A LABORER REQUIRED TO EARN HIS PAY COULD BE SHORTENED.

2. MACHINERY REPLACED WORKERS WHO COULD THEN SERVE CAPITALISTS AS A RESERVE ARMY OF UNEMPLOYED. EAGER FOR JOBS THEY WOULD BID WAGES DOWN.

BUT BOTH OF THESE MEASURES WORKED ONLY AS TEMPORARY VICTORIES FOR CAPITALISTS. BECAUSE, AS MARX POINTED OUT BEFORE, MACHINERY DOES NOT CREATE VALUE ONLY LABOR CAN. THEREFORE, WHEN WAGES DROP LOW ENOUGH, CAPITALISTS WILL EAGERLY HIRE CHEAP LABOR BUT WHEN WAGES RISE AGAIN, CAPITALISTS MUST RESORT TO EVER NEWER INDUSTRIAL TECHNOLOGY. ALL OF WHICH CREATES A DANGEROUS CYCLE.

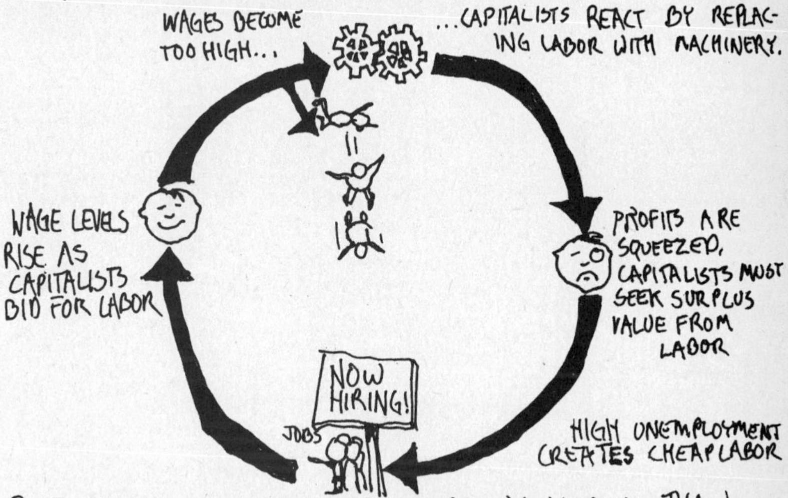

BUT EACH CYCLE BECOMES MORE DANGEROUS THAN THE LAST AS FEWER AND FEWER CAPITALISTS ARE ABLE TO COMPETE, UNTIL ONLY THE BIGGEST, MOST RUTHLESS FIRMS ARE LEFT. BUT THEIR DAY TOO WOULD COME. IN THE END, CAPITALISM WOULD COLLAPSE, PRIVATE PROPERTY WOULD BE ABOLISHED AND THE FACTORS OF PRODUCTION WOULD RETURN TO THE WORKERS.

WHAT KIND OF WORLD WOULD REPLACE CAPITALISM? MARX NEVER OFFERED MUCH BEYOND THE WORD 'COMMUNISM.' HE WAS A REVOLUTIONARY AND AS SUCH HE ONLY SOUGHT THE DESTRUCTION OF THE CAPITALIST SYSTEM, THE ELIMINATION OF PRIVATE PROPERTY AND THE PROFIT MOTIVE AND EVEN AN END TO THE NOTION OF SELF-INTEREST. TO BE REPLACED BY WHAT..? AS MARX PUT IT, "TO EACH ACCORDING TO HIS NEED, FROM EACH ACCORDING TO HIS ABILITY." BUT WHAT DID THIS MEAN, AND HOW WOULD IT ACTUALLY WORK? WE KNOW THAT IN A MARKET SOCIETY, **MONEY**, AND THE ABILITY TO MAKE MONEY, IS THE SOLE DETERMINANT OF WHO GETS WHAT. BUT WHAT WOULD ACT AS A DETERMINANT IN A COMMUNIST SOCIETY? AND WHAT, IF NOT SELF-INTEREST, WOULD COMPEL PEOPLE IN A COMMUNIST SOCIETY TO PRODUCE?

AGAIN MARX OFFERED LITTLE IN THE WAY OF AN EXPLANATION. RATHER, HE LEFT THE JOB OF STRUCTURING COMMUNIST SOCIETY TO ANOTHER. WE'LL SOON LOOK AT THE ARCHITECT OF COMMUNISM AND THE ECONOMIC STRUCTURE WHICH HE DEVISED IN ITS NAME.

THE MARXIST DENTIST
KARL NOT ONLY CONVERTED WORKERS AND INTELLECTUALS TO THE COMMUNIST CAUSE. HE ALSO INSPIRED THIS LONDON DENTIST.
DR. NORMAN CUTLER
1830 - 1898
DR. CUTLER PRACTISED DENTISTRY ONLY TWO DOORS DOWN FROM KARL MARX'S RESIDENCE ON MAITLAND PARK RD. IN LONDON. PRIOR TO CUTLER'S FATEFUL ASSOCIATION WITH MARX, CUTLER'S PRACTICE WAS, BY ALL ACCOUNTS, RESPECTABLE, PERHAPS EVEN PROSPEROUS.
THEIR MEETING WAS NOT ACCIDENTAL. MARX OFTEN SOUGHT CUTLER'S AID IN FINDING A REMEDY TO MARX'S PAINFUL CARBUNCLES. WHEN A GUM BALM PROVED TEMPORARILY SOOTHING, THE TWO SAW MUCH OF EACH OTHER, THOUGH ODDLY MARX PREFERRED TO HAVE HIS DENTAL WORK DONE ELSEWHERE. BUT THIS DID NOT DIM THEIR FRIENDSHIP NOR THEIR SHARED FAITH THAT ONE DAY THE WORLD WOULD BE FREE OF BOTH CAVITIES AND CAPITALISTS.
PHOTO TAKEN AT THE LAUSANNE CONFERENCE BETRAYS A WHIMSICAL SIDE TO THE DOCTOR
CUTLER
MARX
THE FIRST INTERNATIONAL 1867

IN THE FOLLOWING YEARS, DR. CUTLER TOOK MUCH OF THE COMMUNIST POLEMIC TO HEART AND MIND. HE REASONED THAT WHAT WAS TRUE IN THE WORLD OF ECONOMICS MUST ALSO HAVE ITS APPLICATIONS TO DENTISTRY. HE LIKENED MOLARS TO THE OPPRESSED MASSES. AS FOR INCISORS, HE DESPISED THEM. THEY WERE, IN HIS WORDS, "THE WHORE OF TEETH, THE VERY VEIL OF MOLAR DECAY."

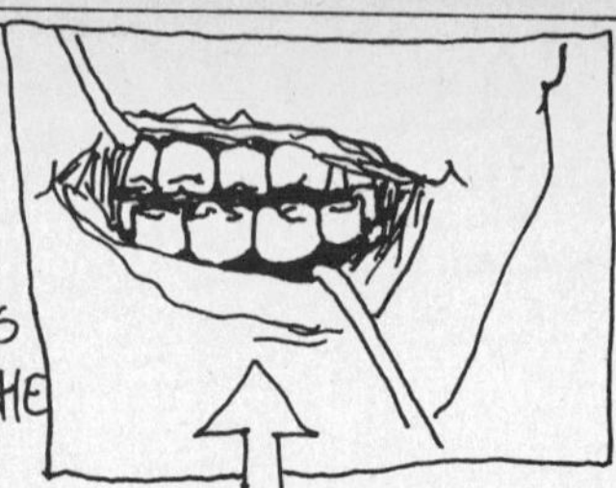

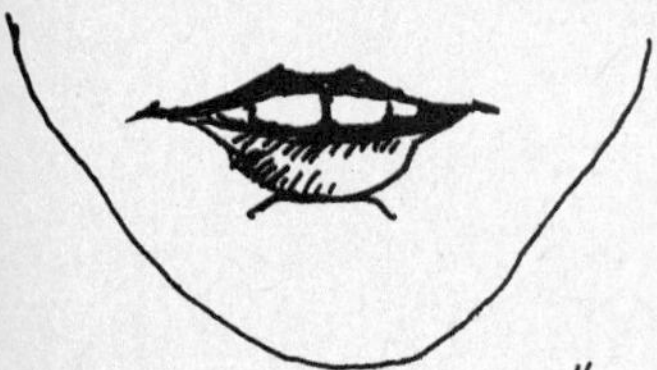

"THE TRULY COMMUNIST MOUTH WOULD CONTAIN MOLARS ALONE," THE MARXIST DENTIST ONCE WROTE. CLEAR AS HIS LOGIC MAY HAVE BEEN, FEW, EVEN THE MOST PROFESSED COMMUNISTS OF THE DAY, WOULD OPEN THEIR MOUTHS TO CUTLER.

"MY METHODS WILL BE PAINFUL, MY PRACTICE WILL BE SMALL," CUTLER ONCE PREDICTED, AND HE WAS RIGHT. CUTLER'S DENTAL IDEOLOGY ATTRACTED FEW ADHERENTS AND HE SOON FOUND HIMSELF WITH EVEN FEWER PATIENTS. BUT, LIKE SO MANY OF HIS FELLOW SOCIALISTS, ADVERSITY ONLY STOKED HIS FLAMES. TO FURTHER DISTANCE HIMSELF FROM THE ORTHODONTIC COMMUNITY, CUTLER PROPOSED RADICAL ORAL SURGERY. THE PROCESS REQUIRED SURGICAL REMOVAL OF ALL THE TEETH FROM THE MOUTH, THEN REIMPLANTING THE TEETH **'RANDOMLY'** BACK INTO THE GUM. (see fig 'B') A HEAVILY DRUGGED AND UNWITTING PATIENT SURVIVED THE PROCEDURE, WHICH WAS TO BE CUTLER'S LAST. HE WAS SOON COMMITTED AND RESTRAINED. DURING HIS TWILIGHT YEARS, HE PENNED AN AUTOBIOGRAPHY. SADLY, THE BOOK WAS NOT EVEN BANNED BY AUTHORITIES. LIKE HIS FAMOUS NEIGHBOR, CUTLER WAS TO DIE POOR & LONELY.

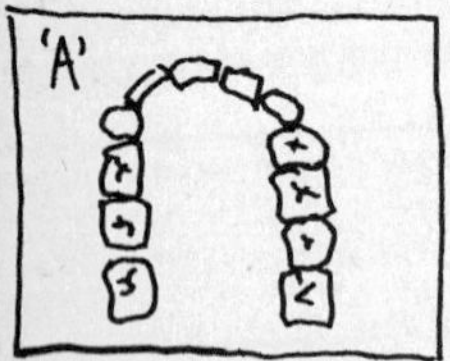

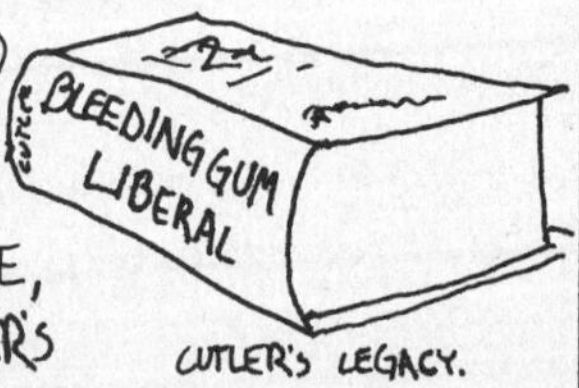

CUTLER'S LEGACY.

MARX LONG CONTENDED THAT SO LONG AS CAPITALISM EXISTED IT WOULD CONTINUE TO HEAP INJUSTICES UPON LABOR AND EXPLOIT WORKERS UNTIL THEY COULD NO LONGER BEAR IT. BUT THIS DID NOT HAPPEN—LABOR REFORMS CAME FIRST. WORKING HOURS WERE REDUCED AND RESTRICTIONS WERE PLACED ON THE HIRING OF WOMEN AND CHILDREN. WHAT BROUGHT ABOUT THESE REFORMS?

UNIONS

LABOR UNIONS UNITED WORKERS AND GAVE THEM A GREAT DEAL OF ECONOMIC AND POLITICAL POWER. WHILE REFORMS BROUGHT BETTER CONDITIONS FOR WORKERS, UNIONS WERE A MAJOR STEP AWAY FROM THE OPEN MARKET.

WITH UNIONS OUR OPEN MARKET BARGAINING TABLE CLEARS OUT CONSIDERABLY AS WORKERS NEGOTIATE WITH JUST ONE VOICE.

NOTE

UNQUESTIONABLY UNIONS CAN BE CREDITED WITH BRINGING ABOUT THE REFORMS WHICH INDIVIDUAL WORKERS WERE POWERLESS TO DO ANYTHING ABOUT, BUT OF VASTLY GREATER IMPORTANCE WAS, AND IS, THE POLITICAL SYSTEM OF DEMOCRACY. FOR ALL OF THE CAPITALIST INJUSTICES WHICH MARX SAW BEING HEAPED UPON THE WORKING CLASS, HE NEVER CONSIDERED THE COUNTERBALANCING POWER FOR CHANGE WHICH CAN BE BROUGHT ABOUT BY THE AROUSED POPULACE OF A DEMOCRATIC SOCIETY. EVERY CRISIS AND INJUSTICE, FROM EARLY WORKER ABUSE TO THE MORE RECENT CRISIS OF POLLUTION, HAS HAD TO AND MUST CONTINUE TO FACE AND SATISFY THIS POWER.

WE WILL COME BACK TO UNIONS LATER IN OUR STORY, PARTICULARLY AS THEY EMERGED IN THE U.S. BUT FOR NOW, WE'LL CONTINUE TO LOOK AT CAPITALISTS AND THEIR ONGOING STRUGGLE TO FREE THEMSELVES FROM THE COMPETITIVE NATURE OF THE MARKET AND THE NEWLY FOUND POWER OF THE LABOR UNIONS.

THIS SHIFTING OF POWER RANKLED EARLY CAPITALISTS, WHO VIEWED PRICE FIXING AS THEIR OWN SACRED DOMAIN. BUT DISTRESSED AS THEY WERE, CAPITALISTS COULD DO NOTHING TO STOP THE SPREAD OF UNIONS ACROSS INDUSTRIAL EUROPE.
UNIONS ARE A THING OF THE DEVIL!
THEY DESTROY THE FREEDOM OF THE OPEN MARKET!
IF ONLY THERE WERE A PLACE WHERE COMPETITION STILL EXISTED!
"GIVE ME YOUR NON-MARXIST, NON UNION... YOUR UNEMPLOYED MASSES WILLING TO WORK FOR SUBSISTENCE WAGES..."

OUR STORY SHIFTS TO THE UNITED STATES. A COUNTRY BETTER SUITED TO CAPITALISM CANNOT BE IMAGINED. WHEN THE INDUSTRIAL REVOLUTION SPREAD ACROSS THE ATLANTIC AN ENDLESS STREAM OF IMMIGRANT LABOR FOLLOWED CLOSELY BEHIND.
WHEN EUROPEAN CAPITALISTS SOUGHT TO EXPAND THEIR MARKETS THEY TREKKED INTO EVEN THE MOST REMOTE CORNERS TO ESTABLISH OUTPOSTS. AMERICA, HOWEVER, CAME READY-MADE WITH ITS OWN SEEMINGLY ENDLESS FRONTIER.
WELL, SIR, HERE YOU ARE; ONE FULLY EXPANDABLE, RUGGEDLY INDEPENDENT, DECIDEDLY ANTICOMMUNIST, CAPITALIST DOMAIN.
AHH, JUST AS I ORDERED... FRONTIERS INCLUDED..?
YES, SIR, FRONTIERS INCLUDED, SHE'S READY FOR EXPANSION.
GOOD! I HATE LIKE HELL TO HAVE TO GO OUT IN SEARCH OF NEW FRONTIERS.
EU

INDEED, FOR CAPITALISTS, AMERICA WAS THE PROMISED LAND. THERE WEREN'T MANY LABOR UNIONS AND THERE WOULDN'T BE UNTIL THE 1930'S. THERE WAS NO INCOME TAX (WITH A BRIEF EXCEPTION JUST AFTER THE CIVIL WAR) AND THERE WOULDN'T BE UNTIL WORLD WAR I. NOW IF THAT WEREN'T ENOUGH, MOST AMERICANS WERE OF THE OPINION THAT THERE WAS A CONNECTION BETWEEN ONE'S WEALTH AND ONE'S GENES. THAT IS - THE RICH WERE RICH BECAUSE THEY WERE OF SUPERIOR STOCK. AND POVERTY SERVED ITS CRUEL PURPOSE BY WEEDING OUT THE INFERIOR STRAINS OF THE HUMAN RACE. SOUND FAMILIAR?

THIS NOTION GOES BACK IN PART TO **MALTHUS**, WHOSE BASIC DOCTRINE WAS MAN'S RELATIONSHIP TO FOOD. SHORTLY THEREAFTER (THOUGH BY NO MEANS BECAUSE OF), CHARLES DARWIN CONCLUDED THAT ALL LIVING THINGS FACED A SIMILAR STRUGGLE FOR SURVIVAL. BUT WHILE DARWIN WAS INITIALLY RETICENT ABOUT LINKING MAN AND EVOLUTION, ANOTHER ENGLISHMAN WAS NOT.

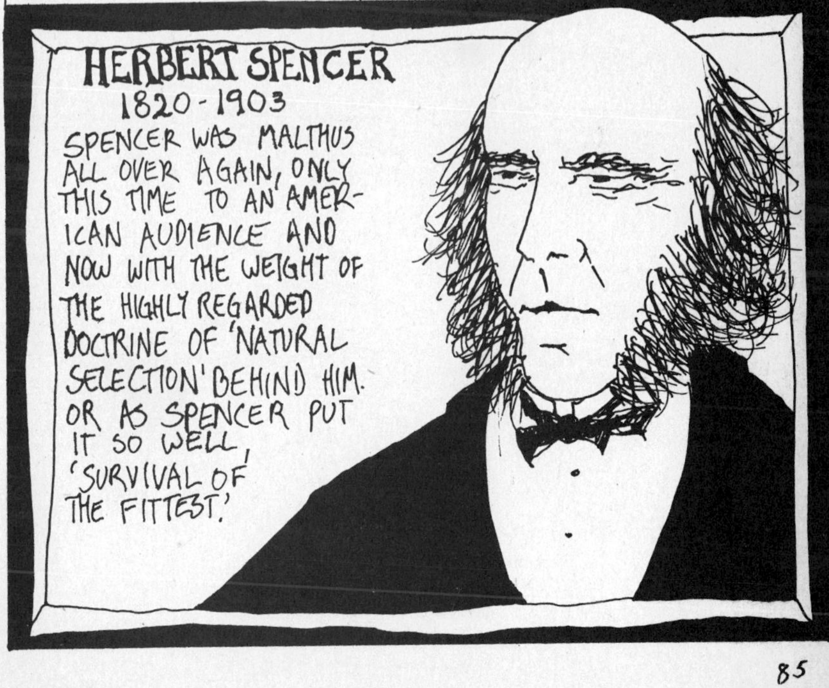

SPENCER SERVED THE TIMES BY RELAYING A MESSAGE THAT MANY, PARTICULARLY WELL-TO-DO AMERICANS, WANTED TO HEAR. WHAT HE TOLD THEM ESSENTIALLY WAS THAT THE AFFLUENT WERE AFFLUENT BECAUSE OF 'NATURAL SELECTION', AND THAT ANY ATTEMPT TO ALTER THAT COURSE, EITHER BY AIDING THE POOR OR CHASTISING THE WEALTHY, MIGHT ONLY UPSET, OR AT LEAST RETARD, THE DELICATE, NATURAL PROCESS BY WHICH A RACE IMPROVES ITSELF.

CONCURRING WITH SPENCER, AS MANY DID, WAS WILLIAM GRAHAM SUMNER, A LEADING ECONOMIST OF THE DAY WHO MANAGED TO COMBINE HERBERT SPENCER, ADAM SMITH AND THE PROTESTANT WORK ETHIC INTO A NEAT PACKAGE, WHEREIN

THE POOR WORKED HARD IN THE STRUGGLE FOR SURVIVAL (AS SELF-INTEREST MIGHT IMPLY) ALONGSIDE THE EQUALLY HARDWORKING (IF SEPARATELY MOTIVATED) RICH. THIS COMBINED EFFORT NOT ONLY PRODUCED GREATER WEALTH, IT ALLOWED MANY MORE TO 'SURVIVE'. AS SUMNER CONCLUDED, "MILLIONAIRES GET HIGH WAGES AND LIVE IN LUXURY, BUT THE BARGAIN IS A GOOD ONE FOR SOCIETY."

ALTHOUGH IT MAY BE HARD TO IMAGINE AMERICAN CAPITALISTS HAVING ANYTHING TO COMPLAIN ABOUT, THERE WAS ONE MATTER THAT PROVED PERSISTENTLY PESKY.
MONEY
AMERICANS HAVE CONTRIBUTED A GREAT DEAL TO WHAT WE KNOW ABOUT THE POSSIBILITIES OF MONEY. THE MOST NOTABLE EXAMPLE IS THE INVENTION OF PAPER MONEY.
WHAT'RE YOU LOOKIN' FOR?
PAPER, NOT BACKED BY GOLD, THAT PEOPLE WILL ACCEPT AS MONEY.
RIGHT UP TO THE AMERICAN REVOLUTION, GOVERNMENTS PAID FOR THE COSTS OF WAGING WAR BY LEVYING NEW TAXES AND/OR BORROWING HUGE SUMS OF MONEY FROM LARGE LENDERS. BUT THE REBELLIOUS COLONISTS DEVISED A NEW APPROACH. THEIR PLAN WAS SIMPLE - PRINT UP PAPER, DECLARE IT LEGAL TENDER, THEN GO OUT AND SPEND IT, BUYING WHAT IS NEEDED.
WELL, JOHN, UNLESS YOU'VE ANY BETTER IDEAS, PUT YOUR HANCOCK HERE.

IT'S DIFFICULT ENOUGH AS IT IS FOR ANY GOVERNMENT TO RAISE MONEY, LET ALONE A REVOLUTIONARY ONE THAT HAS NO WAY TO COLLECT TAXES, EVEN HARDER WHEN THE REVOLUTION IS PROMPTED BY A CERTAIN DISTASTE FOR TAXES. SO LUCKILY FOR THE COLONISTS THERE WAS BEN FRANKLIN. NOT ONLY DID HE ADVOCATE THE USE OF PAPER MONEY, HE WAS WILLING TO SACRIFICE HIS PRINTING PRESS FOR THE CAUSE.

THE FIRST AMERICAN NOTES, 'CONTINENTAL NOTES', WERE NO LESS SIGNIFICANT THAN THE MINUTEMEN OR THE LIBERTY BELL IN SEEING TO THE SUCCESS OF THE REVOLUTION. THEY BOUGHT THE GOODS AND PAID THE TROOPS WHEN NOTHING ELSE WOULD HAVE. BUT AS THE CONTINENTAL CONGRESS PRINTED MORE AND MORE PAPER MONEY, PRICES BEGAN TO RISE. INFLATION SET IN, FOLLOWED BY HYPERINFLATION. THE INITIAL INFLATION OCCURRED SIMPLY BECAUSE AS CONTINENTAL NOTES CIRCULATED, MORE PEOPLE HAD MORE MONEY AND THEY BID THE PRICES OF GOODS UP. AS PRICES WENT HIGHER, THE PEOPLE WHO RECEIVED THE NOTES WANTED MORE IN ANTICIPATION OF EVEN HIGHER PRICES TO COME.

INFLATION OF THIS SORT BECOMES A VICIOUS DOWNWARD CYCLE. AS PEOPLE BEGIN TO DOUBT THE VALUE OF A CURRENCY ITS BUYING POWER IS SURE TO FALL.

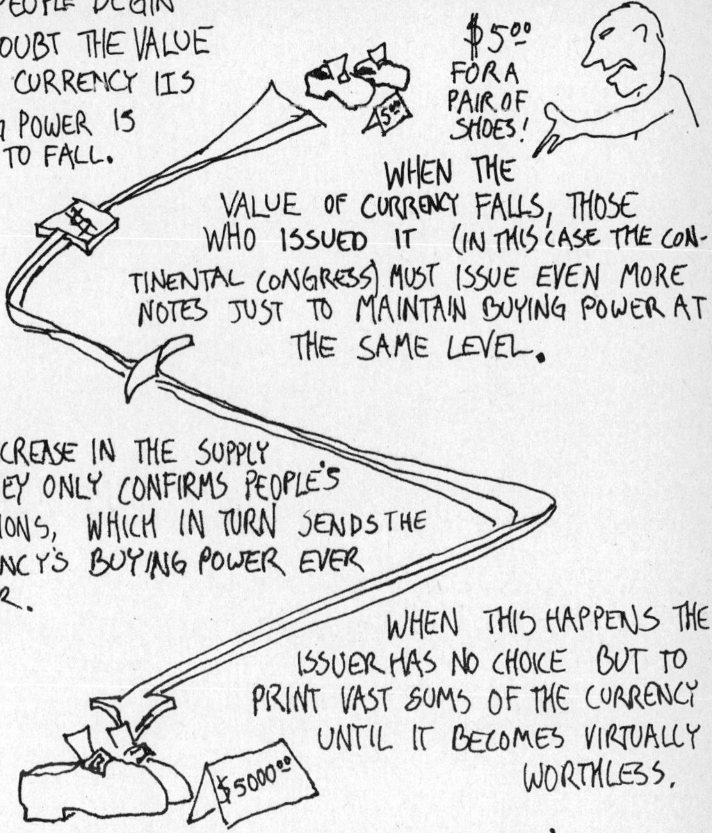

WHEN THE VALUE OF CURRENCY FALLS, THOSE WHO ISSUED IT (IN THIS CASE THE CONTINENTAL CONGRESS) MUST ISSUE EVEN MORE NOTES JUST TO MAINTAIN BUYING POWER AT THE SAME LEVEL.

THIS INCREASE IN THE SUPPLY OF MONEY ONLY CONFIRMS PEOPLE'S SUSPICIONS, WHICH IN TURN SENDS THE CURRENCY'S BUYING POWER EVER LOWER.

WHEN THIS HAPPENS THE ISSUER HAS NO CHOICE BUT TO PRINT VAST SUMS OF THE CURRENCY UNTIL IT BECOMES VIRTUALLY WORTHLESS.

BY WAR'S END, ALEXANDER HAMILTON, THE COUNTRY'S FIRST SECRETARY OF THE TREASURY, AGREED TO REDEEM THE CONTINENTAL NOTES FOR HARD CURRENCY AT THE RATE OF ONE PENNY TO THE DOLLAR. HE THEN ENCOURAGED THE ESTABLISHMENT OF AN AMERICAN CENTRAL BANK ALONG THE LINES OF THE BANK of ENGLAND. THIS BANK WOULD SEE TO A STRONG AND STABLE SUPPLY OF MONEY. INFLATION-WEARY AMERICANS ENDORSED THE IDEA AND IN 1791 THE FIRST BANK of the UNITED STATES WAS CHARTERED.

LIKE THE BANK of ENGLAND, THE FIRST BANK of the U.S. DEMANDED SPECIE (GOLD/SILVER) FOR NOTES OF OTHER AMERICAN BANKS. THIS WAS NOT A PROBLEM IN THE EASTERN STATES WHERE THE FEW BANKS WERE WELL ESTABLISHED. BUT AMERICA WAS A FRONTIER COUNTRY AND FRONTIER BANKS TYPICALLY LIKED LENDING MONEY WHETHER OR NOT ANY SPECIE WAS ON HAND.

THIS WAS THE BEGINNING OF AMERICA'S MONEY WAR. A LONG AND SOMETIMES BITTER CONFLICT. FOUGHT BETWEEN THE 'HARD' MONEY MEN OF THE EASTERN ESTABLISHMENT AND THE 'SOFT' MONEY MEN OF THE FRONTIER. THE FRONTIER NEEDED SETTLERS, SETTLERS NEEDED MONEY ON EASY TERMS AND FRONTIER BANKS WERE EAGER TO PRINT SUCH MONEY AND LOAN IT OUT.

1810: THE SOFT MONEY MEN OF THE FRONTIER WON ROUND ONE. CONGRESS DID NOT RENEW THE CHARTER OF THE FIRST BANK OF THE U.S. IN THE NEXT FEW YEARS THE NUMBER OF BANKS (LARGELY FRONTIER) AND SUBSEQUENT SUPPLY OF MONEY HAD MORE THAN DOUBLED. 1816: ROUND TWO. JOHN JACOB ASTOR LED A GROUP OF EASTERN BANKERS WHO WANTED AND GOT A CHARTER FOR A NEW CENTRAL BANK OF AMERICA.

SPECULATION

THERE IS NO DOUBT THAT THE EASY MONEY POLICIES OF FRONTIER BANKS BENEFITTED MANY, PARTICULARLY FARMERS AND OTHER SMALL BUSINESSMEN WHO NEEDED CREDIT TO GET STARTED, BUT THE RELATIVE AVAILABILITY OF MONEY AND ITS TERMS BROUGHT ABOUT A DUBIOUS, THOUGH UNIQUELY AMERICAN, PASTIME.

THE SECOND BANK OF THE UNITED STATES WAS EVERY BIT AS SUCCESSFUL AS THE FIRST BANK AT REGULATING THE COUNTRY'S MONEY SUPPLY AND CONSEQUENTLY WAS JUST AS SUCCESSFULLY OPPOSED. IN 1832, JUST 16 YEARS AFTER IT'S INITIAL CHARTER, ANDREW JACKSON, A FRONTIER PRESIDENT, VETOED THE BILL APPROVED BY CONGRESS TO RENEW THE BANK'S CHARTER.

WITHOUT A CENTRAL BANK TO CALL IN NOTES FOR REDEMPTION, BANKING ACTIVITY AND MONEY SUPPLY SWELLED, PARTICULARLY ON THE FRONTIER WHERE IT SEEMED ANYONE WITH A PRINTING PRESS AND A PORTRAIT OF ANDREW JACKSON COULD OPEN FOR BUSINESS. BY 1865 THERE WERE REPORTED OVER 7000 DIFFERENT BANK NOTES IN CIRCULATION. THAT YEAR CONGRESS LEVIED A 10% TAX ON ALL NEW BANK NOTE ISSUES...

THE EFFECT?

LIKE THE BRITISH BANKERS BEFORE THEM, AMERICAN BANKERS SIMPLY ELIMINATED BANK NOTES AND REPLACED THEM WITH 'DEMAND DEPOSITS' OR AS WE CALL THEM HERE, CHECKING ACCOUNTS. BE IT BANK NOTES OR CHECK BOOKS, IT'S STILL MONEY; THEY DIFFER ONLY BY DEGREE. BANK NOTES MAY CIRCULATE INDEFINITELY, WHEREAS CHECKS ARE SURE TO BE RETURNED. WE'LL EXAMINE CHECKS MORE CLOSELY, LATER.

LIKE MANY OF THE THINGS WE'VE ENCOUNTERED IN ECONOMICS SPECULATION IS SELF-PERPETUATING. AS PEOPLE BEGIN TO SPECULATE, PRICES GO UP; AS PRICES GO UP, MORE PEOPLE SPECULATE, SENDING PRICES EVEN HIGHER. IN THE END THE RESULT IS ALWAYS THE SAME.

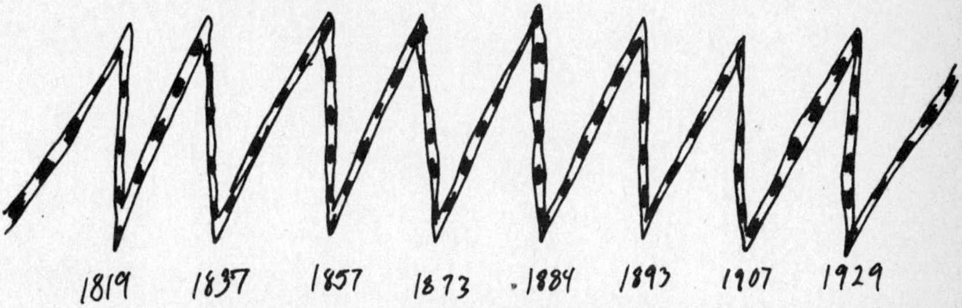

THE DATES REPRESENT PANIC YEARS (PANIC WAS THOUGHT TOO SEVERE A WORD AND WAS REPLACED BY THE WORD 'DEPRESSION,' WHICH IN 1929 OBTAINED A MEANING ALL ITS OWN. TODAY WE CALL SUCH SLUMP YEARS RECESSIONS OR CORRECTIVE GROWTH YEARS). EACH CYCLE IS UNIQUE IN SOME WAY BUT SIMILIAR IN MOST RESPECTS: MONEY BECOMES MORE AVAILABLE, PRICES RISE, BUSINESSES EXPAND, SPECULATION OVERCOMES BETTER JUDGMENT, PRICES PEAK THEN FALL, BUSINESSES FAIL, LOANS DEFAULT, BANKS FAIL, UNEMPLOYMENT LINES FILL, PEOPLE TIGHTEN THEIR BELTS AND PRESIDENTS SPEAK OPTIMISTICALLY.

TRUE, TO SOME EXTENT THESE WERE THE BUSINESS CYCLES WHICH MARX HAD PREDICTED. BUT, WHAT WERE THE EFFECTS OF THESE CYCLES ON THE AMERICAN CAPITALIST SYSTEM? ONE EFFECT, AS MARX FORESAW, WAS THE ELIMINATION OF MANY SMALLER CAPITALISTS SINCE THEY WERE UNABLE TO COPE AS EASILY WITH THE FALLING PRICES BROUGHT ON BY A PANIC. CONSEQUENTLY THE THINKING THEN AMONG AMERICAN CAPITALISTS, AS THEY NEARED THE TWENTIETH CENTURY, WAS IF BIG IS GOOD THEN BIGGER MUST BE BETTER.

TRUE ENOUGH. THE STORY OF AMERICAN CAPITALISTS IS FILLED WITH BOTH THE RUTHLESS AND THE INNOVATIVE. LET'S TAKE A LOOK AT TWO COMMONLY CITED EXAMPLES OF EACH.

TWO AMERICAN CAPITALISTS

JOHN D. ROCKEFELLER

HENRY FORD

ROCKEFELLER GOT STARTED IN BUSINESS JUST IN TIME TO PROFIT FROM THE CIVIL WAR. HE THEN ENTERED INTO THE EMERGING PETROLEUM INDUSTRY, AND THROUGH A COMBINATION OF DRAWBACKS, REBATES AND JUST PLAIN OLD COERCION HE WAS ABLE TO ELIMINATE ALL REAL COMPETITION. HE THEN DEVELOPED THE 'TRUST COMPANY' WHEREIN HE COULD BUY CONTROLLING STOCK IN ANOTHER COMPANY, IN HIS CASE A SUPPLIER OR A POTENTIAL COMPETITOR. EVENTUALLY CONGRESS STEPPED IN WITH ANTITRUST LEGISLATION AND IN 1911 HIS STANDARD OIL COMPANY WAS BROKEN UP.

IN CLASSICAL ADAM SMITH STYLE, HENRY FORD TOOK **'DIVISION OF LABOR'** TO ITS LOGICAL EXTREME ~ THE ASSEMBLY LINE. THE INNOVATION RADICALLY ENHANCED WORKER PRODUCTIVITY, WHICH, IN TURN, ALLOWED FORD TO EMPLOY **ECONOMIES OF SCALE**. HE COULD PURCHASE PARTS AND SUPPLIES IN MASS QUANTITIES, THEREBY LOWERING THE SELLING PRICE OF HIS AUTOMOBILE, MAKING IT AFFORDABLE BY PRACTICALLY EVERYONE. SUCH INNOVATIONS MADE FORD MOTOR COMPANY ONE OF THE LARGEST COMPANIES IN THE WORLD WITH ALMOST ALL OF THAT GROWTH FROM INNOVATION AND INTERNAL GROWTH.

THE B.O.X. SAGA
THIS IS THE ENTIRELY FICTIONAL ACCOUNT OF THE BLOCK BROTHERS BOX COMPANY FROM INCEPTION TO PRESENT DAY. THIS STORY, THOUGH ODDLY UNIQUE, IS NOT ALTOGETHER DISSIMILAR TO THAT OF MANY AMERICAN COMPANIES.
PART 1
THE EARLY YEARS 1860-1900
JOHN BLOCK
"A BOX FOR EVERYTHING AND EVERYTHING IN A BOX," PREACHED JOHN BLOCK, WHO FOUNDED THE COMPANY, SAW IT REACH GREAT HEIGHTS THEN WATCHED HELPLESSLY AS IT WAS TAKEN AWAY FROM HIM.
GEN. 'TACOMA' BLOCK
FORCED TO DECLARE BANKRUPTCY AS A PAPERBOY, TACOMA'S FUTURE WAS ALWAYS IN DOUBT. BUT THEN THE CIVIL WAR BROKE OUT AND THE UNION ARMY FOUND A PLACE FOR HIM.
MORRIS OGILVY
FINANCIER, STOCK BROKER, SPECULATOR HE STEPPED IN AND TOOK CONTROL OF THE BLOCK BROS. BOX COMPANY, MADE IT HIS OWN AND MADE IT AN EMPIRE.

HUMBLE BEGINNINGS. WITH SUFFICIENT LUMBER, NAILS, A HAMMER AND A SAW, JOHN HEADED WEST TO PLY HIS TRADE AS A BOX MAKER.
1860. CINCINNATI, OHIO. THE STUNT THAT LAUNCHED A NEW COMPANY.
BOX MAKER FREED!
IN HOPES OF DRAWING ATTENTION TO HIS FLEDGLING BOX SHOP, JOHN WORKED FIERCELY ONE NIGHT BOXING EVERYTHING IN A TWO-BLOCK AREA OF DOWNTOWN CINCINNATI. HE WAS JAILED BUT SOON RELEASED TO A THRONG OF CHEERING TOWNSFOLK WHO SAW THE STUNT AS A MUCH NEEDED PRANK AMIDST THE GROWING TENSION AND TALK OF WAR.
BUT THEN CAME
WAR
THE NATION DIVIDED
WHILE THE CIVIL WAR DIVIDED MANY FAMILIES, IT BROUGHT THE BLOCK BROTHERS BACK TOGETHER. TACOMA, DESPITE HIS MANY FAILINGS, HAPPENED TO BE DRINKING BUDDIES WITH ANOTHER CHRONIC BUSINESS FLOPSTER, ULYSSES S. GRANT. SO AS GRANT'S FORTUNES ROSE THRU THE RANKS OF THE UNION ARMY, SO RAN THE GOOD FORTUNES OF THE

BLOCK BROTHERS. GIVEN COMMAND OF A SMALL UNIT OF OHIO REGULARS, TACOMA PLACED HIS FIRST OF MANY, MILITARY CONTRACTS WITH JOHN'S BOX COMPANY. JOHN WORKED OVERTIME AND EXPANDED OPERATIONS TO FILL THE ORDER.

IT WAS CALLED 'THE BATTLE BOX', BUT TROOPS DUBBED THEM 'MARCHING CASKETS'. INDEED WHEN THEY WERE PUT TO THE TEST A SLAUGHTER ENSUED. WORD OF THE DISASTER SPREAD QUICKLY. INVESTORS RUSHED TO SELL THEIR STOCK IN THE BLOCK BROS. BOX COMPANY. GRANT PRESIDED OVER A HEARING. TACOMA EXPRESSED DISMAY BUT POINTED OUT THAT THE OFTEN DIFFICULT TASK OF CLEARING THE BATTLEFIELD WAS GREATLY CONVENIENCED BY THE BOX. GRANT CONCEDED THE POINT BUT REMOVED TACOMA FROM BATTLEFIELD COMMAND ALL THE SAME. ODDLY* THE NEXT DAY TACOMA WAS PROMOTED TO THE RANK OF GENERAL IN CHARGE OF ALL MILITARY PROCUREMENTS FOR GRANT'S ARMY. BLOCK BROS. BOX CO. STOCK SOARED IN ANTICIPATION OF COMING ORDERS.

A FEW OF THE BOXES MADE FOR THE UNION ARMY BY THE BLOCK BROS. BOX CO.

SOAP BOX (SET OF FIVE TO ACCOMMODATE DEPLETION)

* THE POINT IS DISPUTED, BUT SOME HISTORIANS CONTEND THAT TACOMA'S PROMOTION WAS LINKED TO A LARGE BLOCK BROS. STOCK PURCHASE MADE THE DAY BEFORE BY AN ASSOCIATE OF GRANT'S BROTHER.

1864 IS THE HIGH-WATER MARK FOR PROUD JOHN BLOCK AND THE BLOCK BROS. BOX COMPANY. AS THE WAR WOUND DOWN, SALES SLUMPED AND INVENTORY BACKED UP. DESPERATE, TACOMA TRIED TO PERSUADE GRANT TO EXTEND GEN. SHERMAN'S 'MARCH TO THE SEA.
SEND HIM ACROSS THE ATLANTIC. HELL, ENGLAND WAS SYMPATHETIC TO THE REBS... LET'S MAKE 'EM PAY FOR IT! ALL YOU'VE GOT TO DO IS CHANGE THE NAME A LITTLE... CALL IT SHERMAN'S MARCH TO THE NORTH SEA!
UNABLE TO CONVINCE GRANT AS TO THE MERITS OF PROTRACTED WARFARE, TACOMA CHOSE TO TAKE MATTERS INTO HIS OWN HANDS. HE PROVISIONED A SMALL ARMADA AND PLUNDERED 'REBEL SYMPATHIZERS' WHEREVER HE COULD FIND THEM ON THE HIGH SEAS. THEN IN 1868 HIS CIVIL WAR DAY ENDED UNCEREMONIOUSLY WHEN HE WAS HUNG AS A PIRATE.
MEANWHILE
HAVING NEGLECTED HIS OLD CUSTOMERS DURING THE WAR YEARS, JOHN BLOCK FINDS HE HAS LOST MUCH GROUND TO COMPETITORS. DESPERATE AND SOMEWHAT NAIVE, BLOCK WAS TAKEN IN BY A SCHEME TO SELL BOXES TO THE PRUSSIANS. HE WAS FLEECED BY A WELL-DISGUISED CON ARTIST AND FRIENDS NOW FEAR THAT HE IS SURE TO LOSE THE COMPANY.
THE DUKE

1869. WALL STREET. BLACK FRIDAY.
SELL SELL SELL SELL
JAY GOULD AND ASSOCIATES ATTEMPT TO CORNER THE GOLD MARKET. RUMORS SPREAD, GRANT WAS IMPLICATED, PANIC SENT GOLD PRICES PLUMMETING. WHEN THE DUST CLEARED ONE MAN EMERGED WITH CONTROLLING INTEREST IN THE BLOCK BROTHERS BOX COMPANY.
THE OGILVY YEARS
THE BLOCK BROS. BOX COMPANY WAS NOW KNOWN AS THE BLOCK-OGILVY BOX COMPANY. OGILVY TOOK OVER THE BOARDROOM AND NAMED HIMSELF CHAIRMAN. HE RETAINED JOHN AS PRESIDENT BUT GREATLY REDUCED HIS AUTHORITY. THIS UPSET JOHN.
YOU DON'T KNOW A THING ABOUT MAKING BOXES, NOT A THING!
GOOD, WE'RE EVEN, BECAUSE YOU DONT KNOW A THING ABOUT MAKING MONEY.
OGILVY CONSOLIDATED OPERATIONS, FIRED MOST OF THE STAFF AND WENT ABOUT ELIMINATING COMPETITION IN ANY WAY HE COULD.
CHICAGO
BOX CO. BURNS
NEW YORK
EXPLOSION AT EAST SIDE BOX CO.
HUGE BOX SALE
I'M JOHN BLOCK OF BLOCK OGILVY BOX COMPANY AND WE'RE SELLING BOXES AT PRICES SURE TO PUT THE OTHER GUYS OUT OF BUSINESS

1882, OGILVY FORMED THE BLOCK-OGILVY TRUST CO. AND QUICKLY WENT ABOUT BUYING UP STOCK IN VARIOUS COMPANIES, ALL OF WHICH WERE SUPPLIERS OF RAW MATERIALS TO THE BOX INDUSTRY. THIS EFFECTIVELY ELIMINATED ALL REAL COMPETITION. OGILVY SET BOX PRICES AS HIGH AS HE FELT THE PUBLIC WOULD BEAR

A PORTION OF A POLITICAL CARTOON THAT INCORRECTLY IDENTIFIED JOHN BLOCK AS ONE OF THE INFAMOUS ROBBER BARONS. A PERFECT EXAMPLE OF HOW OGILVY SHREWDLY USED BLOCK TO DIVERT PUBLIC SCORN AWAY FROM HIMSELF AND HIS FAMILY.

– THISTLETHORN –

INDEED, OGILVY AND HIS FAMILY LIVED A LIFE OF UNIMAGINABLE WEALTH. THISTLETHORN, HIS CONNECTICUT STORYBOOK CASTLE WAS JUST ONE OF HIS HOMES AWAY FROM HOME.

WHILE THE WEALTH THAT ACCRUED TO MANY OF AMERICA'S EARLY CAPITALISTS WAS BEYOND FICTION, MOST AMERICANS REMAINED SUPPORTIVE OF CAPITALISTS AND TOLERANT OF THEIR EXCESSES. PERHAPS THIS WAS BECAUSE AMERICANS ARE EAGER FOR CHANGE AND CAPITALISTS WERE BRINGING IN THE FUTURE AT AN UNPRECEDENTED PACE.

BUT THIS PERCEPTION ALTERED ITSELF GRADUALLY AS IT BECAME APPARENT THAT MOST OF THE SO-CALLED 'CAPTAINS OF INDUSTRY' WERE INDUSTRIOUS ONLY SO LONG AS THEY COULD MAKE MONEY...

... AND SPEND IT.
LIKE OUR FICTIONAL MR. OGILVY, THE OPULENCE OF AMERICA'S EARLY CAPITALISTS WAS REMARKABLE, SO MUCH SO THAT IT NOT ONLY DREW ATTENTION AND ENVY, BUT CRITICISM AS WELL.

THORSTEIN VEBLEN WAS AN AMERICAN ECONOMIST TURNED SOCIAL CRITIC, WHOSE FIRST PUBLISHED BOOK, "THE THEORY OF THE LEISURE CLASS", REFERRED TO THE TENDENCY TOWARD VISIBLE DISPLAY OF WEALTH AS 'CONSPICUOUS CONSUMPTION'. PUBLISHED IN 1899, THE BOOK ESTABLISHED VEBLEN AS THE MOST ASTUTE YET ARCANE OBSERVER OF AMERICA'S MANNERS AND MORALS IN HIS DAY.

VEBLEN'S SECOND BOOK, "THE THEORY OF BUSINESS ENTERPRISE," LAID OUT THE BASIS FOR A SCHOOL OF ECONOMIC THOUGHT WHICH, HOWEVER SMALL, WAS VERY INTERESTING. ESSENTIALLY VEBLEN BELIEVED THAT OF ALL THE VARIOUS TASKS WHICH ECONOMIC MAN COULD PURSUE TO PRODUCE WEALTH, THE BUSINESS MAN (OR AS VEBLEN CALLED HIM, 'THE PROFIT SEEKER') WAS THE LEAST ACCEPTABLE BECAUSE HIS FUNCTION WAS TO SABOTAGE SOCIETY!

VEBLEN NOTED THE PARTICULAR DILEMMA BETWEEN THE PROFIT SEEKER AND THE ENGINEER. THE ENGINEER, SAID VEBLEN, WAS INTERESTED ONLY IN IMPROVING THE PERFORMANCE OF THE MACHINE SO THAT MORE AND BETTER GOODS COULD BE PRODUCED FOR THE BETTERMENT OF ALL. WHEREAS THE PROFIT SEEKER WAS A SABOTEUR IN THE SENSE THAT HE SERVED ONLY HIMSELF BY REDUCING THE QUANTITY OF GOODS (SO THAT THE PRICE WOULD BE BID HIGHER) **AND** BY REDUCING THE QUALITY OF GOODS (DESIGNED OBSOLESCENCE).

DESPITE CRITICISMS FROM THE LIKES OF VEBLEN, AMERICAN CAPITALISTS CONTINUED TO EXPAND. THEY DID THIS BOTH BY CREATING NEW INDUSTRIES AND BY COMBINING THEIR EFFORTS TO EXPAND. THESE COMBINED EFFORTS INCLUDED TAKEOVER TACTICS SUCH AS THE TRUST AND THE HOLDING COMPANY, **AND** THE MUCH FRIENDLIER ARRANGEMENT, THE MERGER.

RECORDS SHOW THAT THE MERGER FOUND GREAT ACCEPTANCE WITH MINING AND MANUFACTURING COMPANIES IN THE YEARS 1897-1899.

WHETHER MINING & MANUFACTURING COMPANIES WERE SIMPLY TRYING TO PROTECT THEMSELVES THROUGH SIZE OR MOVING TOWARD MONOPOLY STATUS IS NOT CERTAIN. BUT CLEARLY THESE COMPANIES PERCEIVED THAT IN THE TWENTIETH CENTURY THE ADVANTAGE WENT TO THE BIGGEST.

AN ALL TOO BRIEF TALE TITLED
THE LAND OF MONOPOLY
OR THE LAND THAT COMPETITION FORGOT.
BRACE YOURSELF, JIM, ENGINES ARE OUT. LOOKS LIKE WERE GOINNA HAVE TO DITCH.
O.K. GORDY.
GOOD THING WE JUMPED WHEN WE DID. YOU KNOW WHERE WE ARE?
NOPE.
LOOK, JIM, A MANUFACTURING CONCERN.
LITTLE DID JIM AND GORDY KNOW THAT THEY HAD STUMBLED INTO A LOST LAND UNTOUCHED BY COMPETITION.
SAY, WHO ARE YOU?
I AM YOUR GUIDE, CHAUM.
WELL CHAUM, TAKE US TO A HOTEL, WE NEED TO CLEAN UP.
AT THE HOTEL
WELL GENTLEMEN WILL THAT BE A DOUBLE OR TWO SINGLES?
ONE NIGHT RATES SINGLES $500.00 DOUBLE $900.00
AT THESE RATES? WHAT DO YOU TAKE US FOR?
HOW DO YOU GET AWAY WITH THESE PRICES?
HOTEL
WHAT D'YA MEAN THE ONLY HOTEL AROUND HERE?
FOR ANY HOTEL TO CHARGE THEM KIND OF RATES WOULD BE SURE TO ATTRACT SOME COMPETITION.
COM·PE·TI·TION? I DONT KNOW THIS WORD.

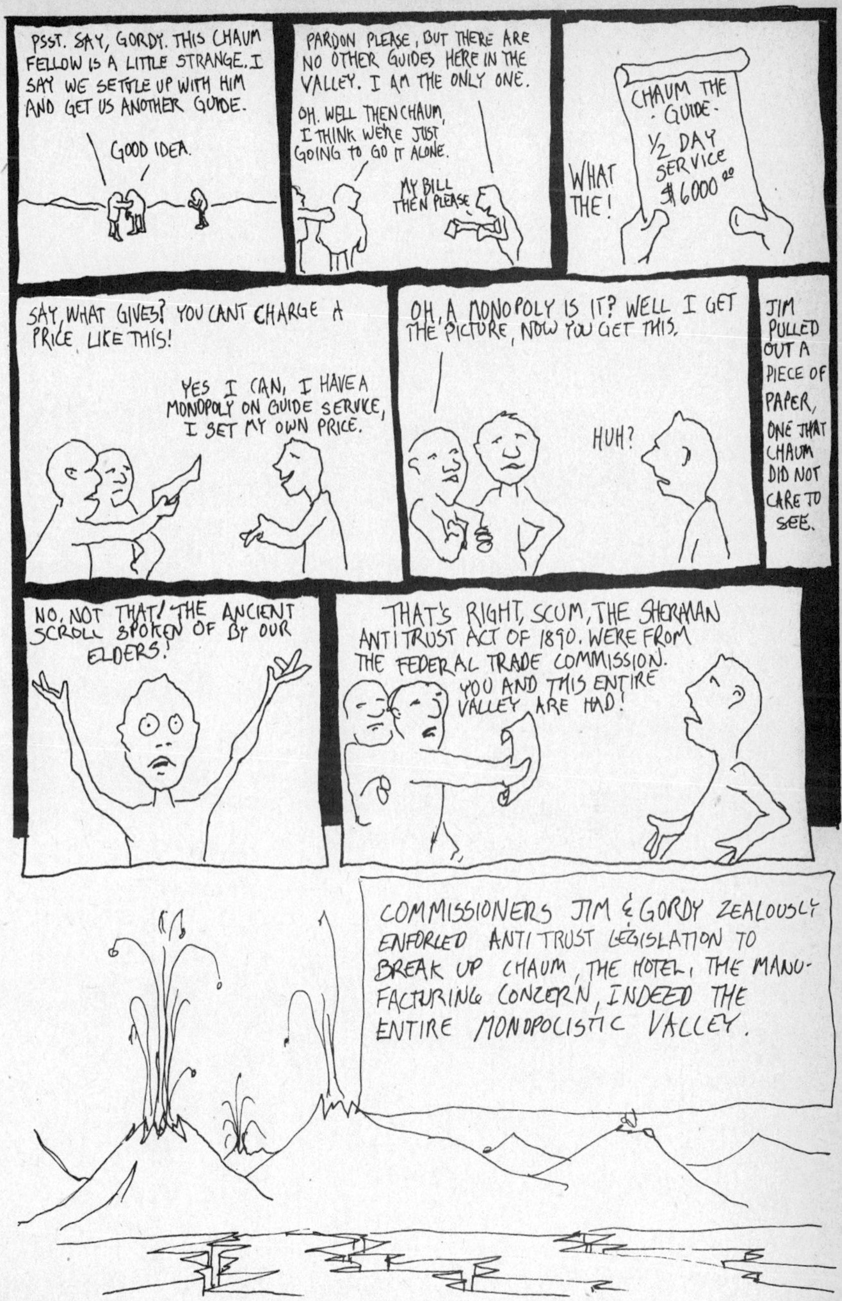
PSST. SAY, GORDY. THIS CHAUM FELLOW IS A LITTLE STRANGE. I SAY WE SETTLE UP WITH HIM AND GET US ANOTHER GUIDE.
GOOD IDEA.
PARDON PLEASE, BUT THERE ARE NO OTHER GUIDES HERE IN THE VALLEY. I AM THE ONLY ONE.
OH. WELL THEN CHAUM, I THINK WE'RE JUST GOING TO GO IT ALONE.
MY BILL THEN PLEASE.
WHAT THE!
CHAUM THE · GUIDE · 1/2 DAY SERVICE $6000.00
SAY, WHAT GIVES? YOU CANT CHARGE A PRICE LIKE THIS!
YES I CAN, I HAVE A MONOPOLY ON GUIDE SERVICE, I SET MY OWN PRICE.
OH, A MONOPOLY IS IT? WELL I GET THE PICTURE, NOW YOU GET THIS.
HUH?
JIM PULLED OUT A PIECE OF PAPER, ONE THAT CHAUM DID NOT CARE TO SEE.
NO, NOT THAT! THE ANCIENT SCROLL SPOKEN OF BY OUR ELDERS!
THAT'S RIGHT, SCUM, THE SHERMAN ANTI TRUST ACT OF 1890. WERE FROM THE FEDERAL TRADE COMMISSION.
YOU AND THIS ENTIRE VALLEY ARE HAD!
COMMISSIONERS JIM & GORDY ZEALOUSLY ENFORCED ANTI TRUST LEGISLATION TO BREAK UP CHAUM, THE HOTEL, THE MANUFACTURING CONCERN, INDEED THE ENTIRE MONOPOLISTIC VALLEY.

THE BANK FAILURE

THE PANIC YEARS WHICH FOLLOWED EACH SUCCESSIVE SPECULATIVE BUSINESS CYCLE ALWAYS ENDED WITH A BANK FAILURE, OR RATHER MANY BANK FAILURES. THE MOST SUSCEPTIBLE BANKS WERE THE SMALLER STATE-CHARTERED OR SO-CALLED 'FRONTIER' BANKS. BUT BY THE 1900'S, AMERICA'S FRONTIERS WERE LARGELY SETTLED AND MANY HOPED THAT STABILITY WAS IN THE OFFING. THIS WAS NOT TO BE. A GREAT DEAL OF SPECULATION WAS BEGINNING TO TAKE PLACE IN THE EAST WITH THE BUYING AND SELLING OF COMPANY STOCKS. THIS SORT OF SPECULATION WAS FINANCED MOSTLY BY 'BANK TRUSTS', A NEW, LESS REGULATED FORM OF BANKING. BUT BEFORE LONG EVERYONE WAS GETTING INTO THE ACT, AND WHEN THE CRASH CAME IN 1907, THE AMERICAN BANKING SYSTEM APPEARED TO BE IN DEEP TROUBLE.

THE PANIC OF 1907 SAW A LOT OF OTHERWISE PROMINENT AMERICANS LOSE MONEY. FOR THIS REASON MORE THAN ANY OTHER, THERE WAS A GREAT CRY IN AMERICA FOR A NEW CENTRAL BANK.

THE FEDERAL RESERVE SYSTEM

WHAT IT IS, WHAT IT ISN'T, WHAT IT DOES, WHAT IT DOESN'T

IT IS NOT A BANK FOR PEOPLE

THE 'FED', AS IT IS AFFECTIONATELY REFERRED TO, DOES NOT ACCEPT DEPOSITS FROM INDIVIDUALS OR LOAN THEM MONEY.

IT IS A BANK FOR BANKERS

LENDING BANKS MAY JOIN THE FEDERAL RESERVE SYSTEM. THEY DON'T HAVE TO, BUT MOST LARGER BANKS DO BELONG.

THE FED IS COMPRISED OF PRIVATE BANKS (MEMBERS) BUT IT IS CONSIDERED A BRANCH OF THE FEDERAL GOVERNMENT AND ITS OFFICERS ARE APPOINTED BY THE PRESIDENT AND CONFIRMED BY THE SENATE.

IT IS A BANK FOR GOVERNMENT

WHEN THE GOVERNMENT NEEDS TO RAISE MONEY BEYOND WHAT IT CAN RAISE IN TAXES IT SELLS SECURITIES. WHEN THE FED BUYS THESE SECURITIES IT IS IN EFFECT LOANING THE GOVERNMENT MONEY.

THE FED IS RESPONSIBLE FOR CONTROLLING THE MONEY SUPPLY

SINCE MOST OF THE LARGER BANKS IN THE COUNTRY BELONG TO THE FEDERAL RESERVE SYSTEM, CERTAIN ACTIONS WHICH THE FED CAN TAKE WILL HAVE A SIGNIFICANT EFFECT ON THE SUPPLY OF MONEY. THE FED CAN CONTROL THE MONEY SUPPLY IN ONE OF AT LEAST THREE WAYS.

1. THE DISCOUNT RATE

IF YOU'LL RECALL FROM OUR EARLIER DISCUSSION OF THE BANK OF ENGLAND, THE DISCOUNT RATE (OR AS THE BRITISH CALL IT, 'THE BANK RATE') IS SIMPLY THE RATE OF INTEREST THAT THE FED CHARGES TO MEMBER BANKS WHEN A BANK NEEDS TO BORROW TO EXPAND LOANS OR COVER DEPOSITS.

IF THE FED CHARGES THEIR MEMBER BANKS A DISCOUNT RATE OF SAY → **8%** → THEN WHEN THE BANK, IN TURN, LOANS THAT MONEY OUT TO ITS CUSTOMERS IT MUST CHARGE A SLIGHTLY HIGHER INTEREST RATE OF SAY → **11%**

NOW IF THE FED LOWERS THE DISCOUNT RATE TO SAY → **5%**

THEN BANKS, IN TURN, CAN CHARGE THEIR CUSTOMERS A LOWER RATE. **8%** THE FED LOWERS THE DISCOUNT RATE WHEN IT WANTS TO INCREASE THE MONEY SUPPLY.

IF THE FED RAISED THE DISCOUNT RATE FROM 8% UP TO SAY → **12%**

THIS WOULD DISCOURAGE BANKS AND BANK CUSTOMERS FROM BORROWING MONEY, AND WOULD CONSEQUENTLY RESULT IN A REDUCTION OF MONEY IN CIRCULATION.

2. THE RESERVE REQUIREMENT

ALL MEMBER BANKS ARE REQUIRED BY THE FED TO PLACE ON RESERVE A CERTAIN PERCENTAGE OF THEIR TOTAL DEPOSITS WITH THE FED.

LET'S SAY THE RESERVE REQUIREMENT IS SET AT ↗ **25%** IF A BANK HAS TOTAL DEPOSITS FROM CUSTOMERS OF SAY $100,000,000.00 THEN THAT BANK MUST RESERVE $25,000,000.00 WITH THE FED.

THAT MONEY NOT ON RESERVE, THE REMAINING $75,000,000, IS AVAILABLE FOR LOANING OUT BY THE BANK.

NOW IF THE FED WISHES TO INCREASE OR DECREASE THE MONEY AVAILABLE FOR BORROWING IN THE COUNTRY THEY NEED SIMPLY CHANGE THE RESERVE REQUIREMENT UP OR DOWN.

HERE'S HOW

BANKS CREATE MONEY. IT IS WHY SO MANY BANKERS LIKE THEIR JOBS. SOMETIMES A BANKER CAN LIKE HIS JOB TOO MUCH AND THAT IS WHY THE FED IS AROUND... TO MAKE SURE THAT BANKERS DONT LIKE THEIR JOBS TOO MUCH. THE FED SEES TO THAT WITH THE RESERVE REQUIREMENT. SINCE THIS ALL HAS TO DO WITH HOW BANKS CREATE MONEY, LET'S LOOK AT THE PROCESS AGAIN, THE WAY MODERN BANKERS DO IT, AND HOW THE FED WITH ITS RESERVE REQUIREMENT PREVENTS BANKERS FROM LIKING THEIR JOBS TOO MUCH.

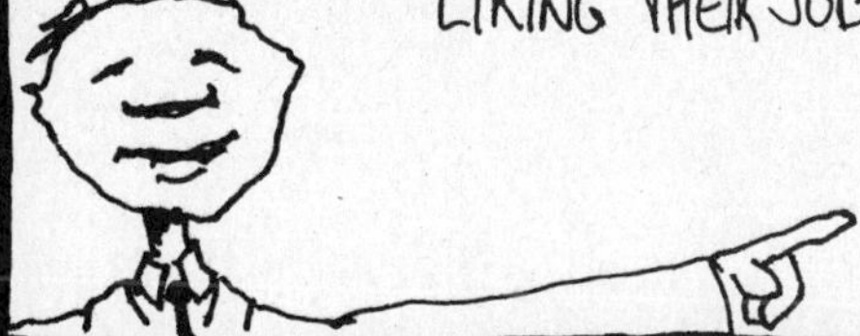

NEXT PAGE...

1
A FELLOW WALKS UP TO A BANK WITH $1000.00. HE WANTS TO OPEN A CHECKING ACCOUNT.
BANK
$
CHECKING ACCOUNTS
LOANS.
CHECKING ACCOUNTS
BANK
LOANS
$
75%
25%
SHIP TO FED
2
HE DEPOSITS THE $1000.00 WITH THE BANK. THE BANK ISSUES HIM A CHECK BOOK WITH A BALANCE OF $1000.00
3
IF THE RESERVE REQUIREMENT OF THE FED IS 25%, THEN THE BANK MUST SET ASIDE $250.00. HOWEVER, THE REMAINING $750.00 IS AVAILABLE TO THE BANK FOR MAKING LOANS.
4
A WOMAN ENTERS THE BANK AND ASKS TO BORROW $750.00. THE BANK APPROVES THE LOAN.
5
5
THE WOMAN TAKES HER BANK LOAN OF $750.00 AND USES IT TO OPEN A CHECKING ACCOUNT. THE BANK NOW HAS A NEW DEPOSIT OF $750.00.
6
AGAIN, THE BANK MUST SET ASIDE 25% OF THIS NEW DEPOSIT, BUT WITH WHAT'S LEFT, IN THIS CASE $562.50, THEY CAN MAKE ANOTHER LOAN. AND WITH ANY LUCK, WHOEVER BORROWS IT WILL REDEPOSIT THE LOAN FOR A CHECKBOOK.
7
ASSUMING THIS HAPPENS, THE BANK CAN ONCE AGAIN LOAN OUT ALL BUT 25% OF THIS NEWLY CREATED DEPOSIT. IN FACT WITH A 25% RESERVE THE BANK CAN CREATE UP TO THREE TIMES THE INITIAL DEPOSIT, OR $3000.00

SAY, ISNT THIS BANKING SYSTEM GREAT? IS THERE ANY DOUBT THAT BANKERS HAVE MORE FUN? THINK ABOUT IT. A GUY WALKS INTO A BANK WITH $1000.00 AND WHEN HE WALKS OUT AGAIN, NOT ONLY DOES HE STILL HAVE HIS $1000.00 (IN THE FORM OF A CHECKBOOK), BUT QUITE A FEW OTHER PEOPLE CAN WALK AWAY FROM THAT BANK A LITTLE RICHER, IF NOT DEEPER IN DEBT.

NOTE: THIS EXAMPLE ASSUMES THAT ALL THIS MONEY (LOANS & DEPOSITS) REMAINS IN THE SAME BANK. OF COURSE THIS NEVER HAPPENS. BUT SO LONG AS ALL THIS MONEY REMAINS IN THE BANKING SYSTEM THE SAME WILL HOLD TRUE IN THE END.

NOW WHAT HAPPENS WHEN THE FED CHANGES THE RESERVE REQUIREMENT?

WE KNOW THAT IF THE RESERVE RATE IS 25% - THEN FOR EVERY $1000.00 WHICH ENTERS A BANK AS MUCH AS $3000.00 CAN BE CREATED BY THE BANKING SYSTEM.

IF THE FED RAISED THE RESERVE RATE TO SAY 50% THEN THE BANKING SYSTEM COULD CREATE NO MORE THAN A $1000.00 FOR EVERY $1000.00 DEPOSITED INTO IT.

CONVERSELY, IF THE FED LOWERED THE RESERVE RATE TO SAY 10% THEN FOR EVERY $1000.00 DEPOSITED INTO THE BANKING SYSTEM ANOTHER $9000.00 COULD BE CREATED!

3. OPEN MARKET OPERATIONS

WHILE THE FED ALTERS THE RESERVE REQUIREMENTS ON OCCASION TO AFFECT THE NATION'S MONEY SUPPLY, THEY DO NOT ALTER IT VERY OFTEN. FOR DAY-TO-DAY FINE TUNING OF THE ECONOMY, THE FED LIKES TO PLAY AROUND WITH SOMETHING THEY CALL OPEN MARKET OPERATIONS. THIS IS A VERY SIMPLE PROCEDURE AND EASY TO UNDERSTAND.

SUPPOSE THAT

LET'S SAY, FOR CONSISTENCY'S SAKE, THAT THE RESERVE RATIO IS SET AT 25% AND EVERYONE WANTS TO LEAVE IT RIGHT THERE...BUT... THINGS ARE JUST A LITTLE SLUGGISH IN THE ECONOMY, AND THE FED WANTS TO SPARK THINGS UP A BIT!

OUR EXAMPLE

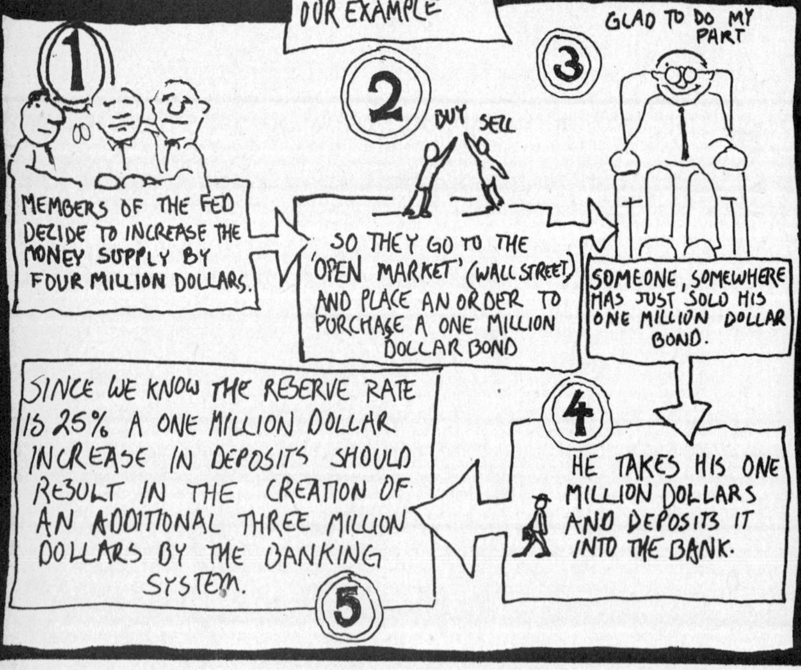

HOW THE THREE STEPS WORK TOGETHER
AN ILLUSTRATED EXAMPLE
THE RESERVE REQUIREMENT IS LOW (LET'S SAY 10%). THIS MEANS THAT AS DEPOSITS COME IN - BANKS FIND THAT THEY CAN MAKE A LOT OF MONEY, LITERALLY!
SOMEONE BORROW PLEASE!
THIS MEANS THAT BANKERS WANT TO LOAN MONEY.
INTEREST RATES FALL AS BANKS COMPETE TO LOAN MONEY. PEOPLE BEGIN TO BORROW MORE MONEY. THIS CREATES AN INCREASE IN THE MONEY SUPPLY WHICH RESULTS IN HIGHER PRICES,
WHICH LEADS TO INFLATION.
PEOPLE HATE INFLATION. IT MEANS THERE'S NO TELLING WHAT THEIR MONEY WILL BUY TOMORROW.
PEOPLE WRITE ANGRY LETTERS TO THEIR CONGRESSMEN. HEARINGS ARE HELD AND POSTULATIONS MADE, AND ALL AGREE THAT SOMETHING MUST BE DONE.
IN STEPS THE FED!
FIRST THING THE FED DOES IS TO RAISE THE RESERVE REQUIREMENT AND UP THE DISCOUNT RATE.
NEXT THE FED SELLS HUGE AMOUNTS OF BONDS AND SECURITIES ON THE OPEN MARKET.
BANK DEPOSITS (AND RESERVES) ARE DEPLETED WHEN PEOPLE BUY THESE BONDS FROM THE FED. TO REPLENISH THEIR RESERVES BANKS MUST BORROW MONEY FROM THE FED. WITH THE DISCOUNT RATE HIGH AND THE AVAILABILITY OF LENDABLE MONEY DIMINISHED, INTEREST RATES WILL SOAR CAUSING PEOPLE TO STOP OR SLOW THEIR BORROWING OF MONEY.
THE RESULT? WITH LESS LOANS GOING OUT, LESS MONEY WILL BE CIRCULATING. THIS WILL CAUSE PRICES TO FALL AND INFLATION WILL GO AWAY. CLEARLY THE FED HAS SOME POWERFUL TOOLS TO AFFECT THE NATION'S ECONOMY. LET'S GET BACK TO THE STORY AND SEE HOW THEY USED THESE TOOLS.

1914 THE FED IN ACTION

1914 WAS A SEEMINGLY GOOD YEAR FOR AMERICA. IT WAS THE YEAR THAT SAW THE CREATION OF THE FEDERAL TRADE COMMISSION AND PASSAGE OF THE CLAYTON ANTITRUST ACT. BOTH WERE DESIGNED TO STEM THE MONOPOLISTIC TENDENCIES OF AMERICAN CAPITALISTS. FINANCIALLY, THERE WAS CAUSE FOR HOPE. AMERICA WAS ON THE GOLD STANDARD, MEANING AMERICAN CURRENCY WAS NOW LIKE EUROPEAN CURRENCIES IN THAT IT WAS BACKED BY GOLD. AND FINALLY 1914 WAS THE YEAR THAT THE FEDERAL RESERVE BOARD WAS FOUNDED. THEIR FUNCTION, IT WAS HOPED, WOULD BE TO KEEP PRICES STABLE AND GROWTH CONTINUAL.

UNFORTUNATELY, NO SOONER HAD AMERICA PULLED ITSELF TOGETHER THAN DID EUROPE BEGIN TO TEAR ITSELF APART. WAR BROKE OUT IN 1914 AND THE FIRST THING THE WARRING EUROPEAN NATIONS DID WAS TO TAKE THEIR CURRENCIES OFF THE GOLD STANDARD.

WHEN THE EUROPEANS WENT OFF THE GOLD STANDARD THE FLOOD OF GOLD INTO THE UNITED STATES WAS GREATER THAN WHAT FLOODED SPAIN IN THE 1500'S. THE POTENTIAL FOR INFLATION WAS ENORMOUS. WHAT DID THE FED DO? DID THEY RAISE THE RESERVE REQUIREMENT. NO, ACTUALLY THEY LOWERED THE DISCOUNT RATE. WHY? BECAUSE THE AMERICAN ECONOMY WAS EXPANDING RAPIDLY. GOLD WAS COMING INTO THE U.S. NOT JUST FOR SAFEKEEPING BUT TO BUY AMERICAN PRODUCTS, GRAIN AND MATERIAL. AMERICANS WERE ALSO CONSUMING LESS, FOR TWO REASONS. FIRST, IN 1914 AMERICANS BEGAN PAYING AN INCOME TAX AND LATER IN 1917 WHEN AMERICA ENTERED THE WAR AMERICANS WERE URGED TO PURCHASE WAR BONDS.

WHEN PEOPLE BUY BONDS THEY REDUCE THE AMOUNT OF MONEY THEY HAVE TO SPEND ON CONSUMER GOODS. IT'S A FORM OF SAVINGS THAT PERMITS A GOVERNMENT TO REDIRECT MONEY, CAPITAL AND MANPOWER INTO THE BUILDING OF MILITARY CAPITAL AND GOODS. BUT DESPITE BONDS AND THE INCOME TAX, PRICES CONTINUED TO RISE. BY 1917, IN THE SPACE OF A FEW SHORT YEARS, AMERICAN WHOLESALE PRICES HAD DOUBLED. BEFORE WE CONTINUE, LET'S TAKE A LOOK AT THE GOLD STANDARD AND HOW IT WAS TO WORK.

THE GOLD STANDARD
GOOD OR BAD?
FOR A TIME, A VERY BRIEF TIME, THE WORLD HAD ARRIVED MONETARILY. GOLD WAS, IN A SENSE, AN INTERNATIONAL CURRENCY IN THAT ALL CURRENCIES WERE BACKED BY GOLD. WAS THIS GOOD? SHOULD NATIONS RETURN TO THE GOLD STANDARD? WAS IT REALLY SUCH A GOOD IDEA IN THE FIRST PLACE? AND IF IT ISN'T A GOOD IDEA WHY DO MANY PEOPLE URGE A RETURN TO THE GOLD STANDARD? LET'S LOOK AT A SIMPLE EXAMPLE...
LET'S SAY A GREAT DEAL OF GOLD BEGINS TO BUILD UP IN FRENCH BANKS AND IN THE FRENCH TREASURY.
C'EST BON
THIS PROMPTS FRENCH BANKS TO MAKE MORE LOANS. THE FRENCH ECONOMY EXPANDS, PROVIDING MORE JOBS. THIS EXPANSION PUSHES PRICES UP. HIGHER PRICES MEAN THAT FRENCHMEN MAY BEGIN TO BUY CHEAPER GOODS FROM ABROAD, WHILE OTHER NATIONS WILL BUY FEWER FRENCH GOODS BECAUSE THEY ARE HIGHER PRICED...
GOLD LEAVES FRANCE FOR THE OTHER COUNTRIES WHERE GOODS ARE CHEAPER, BRINGING EXPANSION WITH IT. MEANWHILE FRENCH BANKS MUST CURTAIL LOANS, AND THE FRENCH ECONOMY CONTRACTS AS PRICES FALL.
DON'T GO
WHEN PRICES OF FRENCH GOODS FALL AND EXPANSION BRINGS HIGHER PRICES TO OTHER COUNTRIES THEN THE INEVITABLE HAPPENS, GOLD FLOWS BACK TO FRANCE AND EXPANSION RESUMES.
YOU'RE BACK!
BUT THIS PROCESS WORKS MUCH THE SAME WAY TODAY WITHOUT THE GOLD STANDARD! SO WHAT'S THE DIFFERENCE? WITH GOLD, EXPANSION AND CONTRACTION ARE DEPENDANT ONLY ON THE SUPPLY OF GOLD IN A COUNTRY. WITHOUT THE GOLD STANDARD, POLITICIANS ARE FREE TO INTERCEDE AND MAKE CORRECTIONS. WITH GOLD, AN ECONOMY THAT WANTS TO EXPAND MAY NOT BE ABLE TO IF GOLD RESERVES ARE LOW. ALSO A GOLD STANDARD FORCES A SORT OF ACCOUNTABILITY OF ALL NATIONS TO EACH OTHER. WITHOUT THE GOLD STANDARD, POOR ECONOMIC JUDGMENTS MADE BY ONE NATION CAN HARM, NOT HELP, OTHER NATIONS.

IN 1917 THE FLOW OF GOLD BEGAN TO RESPOND TO HIGH-PRICED AMERICAN GOODS AND MOVE ON TO OTHER NEUTRAL NATIONS. BUT BEFORE THIS GOT OUT OF HAND THE UNITED STATES ENDED ITS BRIEF ASSOCIATION WITH THE GOLD STANDARD. (AMERICAN CURRENCY WAS STILL BACKED BY GOLD BUT GOLD COULD NOT, BY LAW, LEAVE THE COUNTRY.) MAINTAINING HUGE GOLD RESERVES, THE U.S. THEN MADE LOANS AVAILABLE TO THE ALLIED NATIONS.

THESE LOANS KEPT DEMAND AND PRICES HIGH FOR AMERICAN GOODS THROUGHOUT THE WAR AND EVEN FOR A FEW YEARS BEYOND. BUT BY 1920 DEMAND HAD FALLEN CONSIDERABLY. THE ONLY THING LEFT WAS FOR PRICES TO FALL. THE RESULTING DEPRESSION WAS BRIEF BUT SEVERE.

AND WHAT DID THE FED DO? THE FED RAISED THE DISCOUNT RATE TO 6%. THIS WAS UNUSUALLY HIGH FOR THAT TIME) AND MEANT THAT BANKS WOULD HAVE TO CHARGE AN EVEN HIGHER RATE TO THEIR CUSTOMERS. NATURALLY THE RESULT WAS A SHARP DROP IN THE NUMBER OF BANK LOANS AND A DEEPENING OF THE DEPRESSION.

IT IS WORTH NOTING THE DISPARITY IN THE WAY PRICES WERE FALLING AT THAT TIME. PRICES OF FARM PRODUCTS FELL DRASTICALLY AND STAYED LOW WHEREAS PRICES OF INDUSTRIAL GOODS REMAINED MUCH CLOSER TO THE WARTIME LEVELS. WHY..?

MONOPOLY

WHEAT PRICES ARE OFTEN USED BY ECONOMISTS AS AN EXAMPLE OF 'NEAR PERFECT COMPETITION.' THAT IS, NUMEROUS SELLERS, IN THIS CASE FAMILY FARMERS, COMPETING AGAINST EACH OTHER MUST SELL THEIR PRODUCTS AT THE LOWEST PROFITABLE PRICE. WHILE NEAR PERFECT COMPETITION WAS RIGOUROUSLY APPLIED TO CERTAIN SEGMENTS OF THE ECONOMY, BY 1921 IT WAS CLEAR THAT IT DID NOT APPLY TO EVERYONE. INDUSTRIALISTS WERE ESCAPING FROM THE MARKET AND IT WAS NOW APPARENT THAT THEY WERE EXERTING SOME CONTROL OVER THEIR PRICES. SO WHAT ABOUT THE ANTITRUST ACTS AND THE F.T.C.? WHILE THEIR POWER WAS STILL INTACT NO ONE WAS VIGOROUSLY EXERCISING IT. THE ATTITUDE THEN AND THROUGHOUT THE 1920'S WAS THAT WHEN THINGS WERE GOOD, LEAVE WELL ENOUGH ALONE AND IT SEEMED TO EVERYONE THAT THE 20'S WERE NOTHING BUT GOOD.

1923-1929
PROMISE of PROSPERITY
PRELUDE to DISASTER
FREE LUNCH

THE 1920'S BROUGHT ON TWO OF THE MOST DRAMATIC EXAMPLES TO DATE OF MONEY'S FAILINGS. IN ONE CASE, IN 1923, GERMAN MONEY BECAME WORTHLESS BECAUSE EVERYONE SPENT ALL THAT THEY HAD AS SOON AS THEY GOT IT. IN THE SECOND CASE, LESS THAN A DECADE LATER, AMERICAN MONEY FAILED BECAUSE EITHER YOU DIDN'T HAVE IT TO SPEND OR IF YOU HAD ANY YOU DIDN'T WANT TO SPEND IT.

FIRST TO GERMANY

ALL OF THE EUROPEAN COUNTRIES HAD INFLATION TO SOME DEGREE DURING WORLD WAR I, THE WINNERS AND THE LOSERS. MUCH OF THE CAUSE FOR INFLATION LAY NOT SO MUCH WITH THE DESTRUCTION OF WAR BUT RATHER WITH HOW MUCH PAPER MONEY THE RESPECTIVE GOVERNMENTS HAD PRINTED TO PAY FOR THE WAR. IN COMPARISON, GERMANY'S INFLATION DURING THE WAR WAS MODEST. BUT AFTER THE WAR IT DIDN'T LET UP. THE NEWLY FORMED GOVERNMENT DIDN'T HELP. IT COULD BARELY ENFORCE ORDER MUCH LESS COLLECT TAXES SO IN CONSEQUENCE THE GOVERNMENT BORROWED MONEY TO MEET EXPENSES. IT GAVE GERMANS A DISLIKING FOR INFLATION WHEN IN 1919 PRICES ROSE THREEFOLD. A CERTAIN MEASURE OF STABILITY APPEARED FEASIBLE IN 1920 AS PRICES LEVELED OFF BUT THEN IN 1921 A NEW THREAT CAME FROM THE VENGEFUL ALLIES.

KNOWING THEY COULD NEVER PAY, GERMANS FEARED RENEWED INFLATION.

INFLATION IS GENERALLY DEFINED BY ECONOMISTS AS TOO MUCH MONEY CHASING TOO FEW GOODS.

WHEN INFLATION BECOMES SEVERE PEOPLE SENSE THAT MONEY WILL BUY EVEN LESS TOMORROW THAN IT DOES TODAY... SO BEST BUY TODAY. IN GERMANY THIS IS PRECISELY WHAT HAPPENED. DISHEARTENED AND UNCERTAIN AS TO THE FUTURE GERMANS NOT ONLY SPENT THEIR CASH ON HAND, THEY LIQUIDATED EVERYTHING THEY HAD IN THE WAY OF SAVINGS (STOCKS, BONDS, PASSBOOKS), THEN FLOODED THE MARKETPLACE WITH MONEY. THIS SENT PRICES SOARING. AS PRICES SHOT UP WAGES SHOT UP AFTER THEM, WHICH ONLY SENT PRICES EVEN HIGHER. PRICES WENT UP BY THE DAY, SOMETIMES BY THE HOUR. BY THE END OF 1922 PRICES WERE NEARLY 1500 TIMES THEIR PREWAR LEVEL. AND WHEN IT ALL CAME TO AN END IN NOVEMBER OF 1923, PRICES WERE RUNNING ONE TRILLION, FOUR HUNDRED AND TWENTY-TWO BILLION, NINE HUNDRED MILLION TIMES THEIR 1914 LEVEL. AT THAT TIME A NEW MARK WAS INTRODUCED WHICH COULD BE TRADED FOR ONE TRILLION OF THE OLD BY THE GERMAN CENTRAL BANK.

BACK TO AMERICA AND THE FLIP SIDE OF THE COIN

AMERICA'S GREAT DEPRESSION WAS PRECEDED BY A SUSTAINED AND SPECTACULAR STOCK MARKET BOOM. WHILE AMERICA'S HISTORY OF SUCH BOOM AND BUSTS WAS WELL RECORDED EVEN THEN, THE PREVAILING WIZARDS OF THE DAY (THE FED IN PARTICULAR) PROVED THEMSELVES REMARKABLY IGNORANT.

THE BOOM

THE 1920'S HAVE BEEN PICTURED AS AN ERA OF GREAT PROSPERITY FOR AMERICA. IN TRUTH THIS WAS NOT QUITE ACCURATE. FOR THE AMERICAN FARMER TIMES WERE DESPERATELY BAD. WHEN THE WAR ENDED FARM PRODUCTS GLUTTED THE MARKET. THIS SENT PRICES DOWN LOW, WHERE THEY STAYED.

FOR THE FACTORY WORKER THINGS WERE ONLY A LITTLE BETTER. WHILE THE ASSEMBLY LINE AND OTHER TECHNOLOGICAL INNOVATIONS WERE VASTLY IMPROVING WORKER PRODUCTIVITY DURING THE TWENTIES, WAGE LEVELS STAYED NEARLY CONSTANT. AND YET FALLING PRICES (PARTICULARLY FOOD) MEANT THAT MOST WORKERS FELT AT LEAST A MODEST IMPROVEMENT IN THEIR STANDARD OF LIVING.

IF FARMERS AND WORKERS WERE NOT BENEFITTING DURING THE ROARING TWENTIES THEN WHO WAS? WITH THE COST OF LIVING DROPPING, WAGES STAYING CONSTANT AND WORKER PRODUCTIVITY RISING DRAMATICALLY SOMEONE MUST HAVE BEEN BENEFITTING... BUT WHO?

BEFORE THE CRASH CAME CORPORATE PROFITS HAD DOUBLED - THEN TRIPLED THEIR 1920 LEVEL. AND WHERE WAS THIS MONEY GOING? MOST OF IT WAS GOING BACK INTO INVESTMENT - INTO SAVING AND INTO SPECULATION (THIS PRESENTED A POTENTIALLY SERIOUS PROBLEM WHICH WE'LL LOOK AT VERY SOON). SINCE MUCH OF THIS INVESTMENT AND SPECULATION TOOK PLACE IN THE STOCK MARKET, STOCK PRICES WENT UP. THIS ENCOURAGED OTHERS. PERHAPS ONE OF THE MOST POPULAR WAYS OF INVESTING IN THE STOCK MARKET WAS THROUGH THE 1920'S VERSION OF THE MUTUAL FUND KNOWN AS THE INVESTMENT TRUST.

HOW THE INVESTMENT TRUST WORKED

FINANCIERS FORM THE FUD-HALL INVESTMENT TRUST. $100 MILLION IS RAISED FOR INVESTMENT PURPOSES THROUGH THE SALE OF STOCK TO THE PUBLIC. THE MONEY IS EASILY RAISED AND THE VALUE OF FUD-HALL STOCK RISES AS INVESTORS SEEK TO BUY MORE FUD-HALL STOCK

→ FUD-HALL FORMS MID-MALL, ANOTHER INVESTMENT TRUST COMPANY. MID-MALL STOCK IS SOLD QUICKLY. ITS VALUE RISES, AND PROCEEDS RETURN TO FUD-HALL.

→ MID-MALL FORMS BUD-BALL INVESTMENT TRUST. BASED ON THE SUCCESSFUL RISE IN STOCK OF FUD-HALL AND MID-MALL, BUD-BALL STOCK SELLS QUICKLY.

→ BUD-BALL INVESTS IN DACRON POWER & LIGHT. AN ACTUAL INCOME-PRODUCING COMPANY.

THE FRAGILITY OF SUCH INVESTMENT TRUSTS WAS RARELY DISCUSSED. THE IMPORTANT THING WAS THAT PEOPLE WERE CRAZY TO INVEST. IT DIDN'T SEEM TO MATTER IF A COMPANY PRODUCED ANY WEALTH, WHAT REALLY MATTERED WAS WHETHER OR NOT THEIR STOCK WOULD CONTINUE TO RISE.

BUYING ON MARGIN

BUTTER THAN BUYING ON MARGARINE.

NOT ONLY WERE A GREAT MANY INVESTMENT TRUSTS STACKED UP LIKE A HOUSE OF CARDS, MUCH OF THE MONEY WHICH WENT TO PURCHASE THEIR STOCK WAS BORROWED. THAT IS, BANKS AND EVEN COMPANIES LOANED MONEY TO PEOPLE TO SPECULATE IN THE STOCK MARKET. THE STOCKS WERE HELD AS COLLATERAL AND SO LONG AS PRICES CONTINUED TO RISE, EVERYONE WAS HAPPY.

FANNING THE FLAMES WITH THE FED

WHILE ALL SEEMED WELL IN AMERICA, EUROPE IN 1927 WAS AILING. BUSINESS WAS OFF, UNIONS WERE FEISTY AND EUROPEAN INVESTORS SAW BETTER RETURNS FOR THEIR MONEY OVERSEAS. THIS PROMPTED A CONSORTIUM OF EURO-BANKERS TO GO TO NEW YORK AND APPEAL TO THE FED. THEIR SOLUTION WAS SIMPLE. THE FED WAS TO EASE CREDIT, EXPAND THE MONEY SUPPLY. THIS WOULD SEND PRICES OF AMERICAN GOODS UP AND EUROPEAN GOODS WOULD BECOME CHEAPER. IT WAS CLASSIC ECONOMICS.

WHAT HAPPENED?

THE FED COMPLIED. THEY LOWERED THE DISCOUNT RATE, THEN MADE MASSIVE SECURITIES PURCHASES IN THE OPEN MARKET. THIS ACTION FLUSHED BANKS AND EVERYONE (INVESTORS) ELSE WITH CASH. AND IT SENT STOCK PRICES SO HIGH THERE WAS ONLY ONE THING THEY COULD DO.

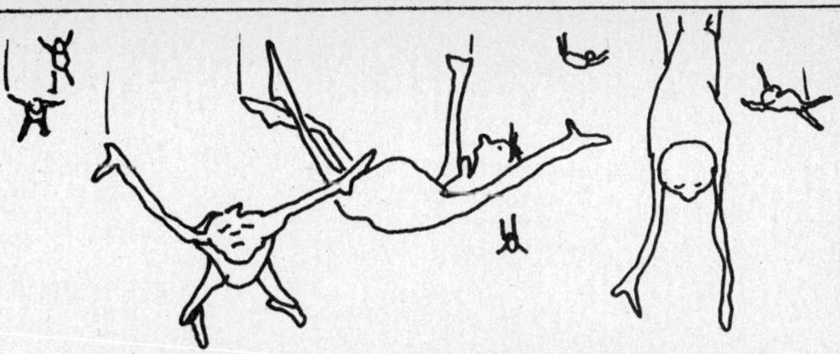

THE CRASH

OCTOBER 29, 1929, THE BOTTOM FELL OUT. IN ONE DAY THE GAINS OF THE ENTIRE YEAR WERE WIPED OUT. TRUSTS, BANKS AND EVEN BUSINESSES, NOT TO MENTION PERSONAL SAVINGS, WERE ALL WIPED OUT. BILLIONS OF DOLLARS OF PAPER WEALTH SIMPLY VANISHED. THE FED, WHO AIDED SPECULATION WITH OPEN MARKET OPERATIONS, WERE FULLY ABLE TO PROP UP STOCK PRICES AND RESCUE BANKS BUT CHOSE INSTEAD TO SUSPEND OPEN MARKET OPERATIONS. BANKS AND BUSINESSES WERE CLOSING BY THE HUNDREDS EVERY DAY. WHEN THE FED RENEWED OPEN MARKET PURCHASES AND LOWERED THE DISCOUNT RATE TO 1.5% IT WAS TOO LATE. ONE FOURTH OF THE WORKFORCE WAS UNEMPLOYED. THOSE THAT HAD JOBS FACED CONTINUAL WAGE CUTS. EVEN WHEN SURVIVING BANKS HAD MONEY TO LEND THEY WERE RELUCTANT TO DO SO. BESIDES, IT SEEMED NO MATTER HOW LOW THE INTEREST RATES WERE, BUSINESSES WEREN'T BORROWING.

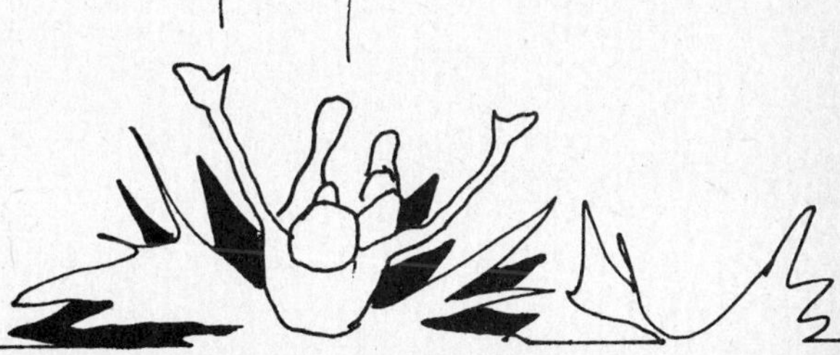

REVIEW

WE KNOW THAT THE MARKET ECONOMY TOOK THE SLOW ROAD TO REALIZATION. THAT IS, THE COMPONENTS OF THE MARKET SOCIETY, OR AS ECONOMISTS CALL THEM, 'THE FACTORS OF PRODUCTION', REQUIRED CERTAIN PRECONDITIONS LIKE PRIVATE PROPERTY (OWNERSHIP OF LAND AND CAPITAL BY PRIVATE ENTITIES), A FREE AND AUTONOMOUS LABOR FORCE AND FINALLY THE PROFIT-SEEKING ENTREPRENEUR TO PUT IT ALL TOGETHER.

THESE PROFIT-SEEKING ENTREPRENEURS, IN COMPETITION WITH OTHER LIKE-MINDED SORTS, SOON DISCOVERED THAT THE COMPETITIVE EDGE WENT TO THOSE ENTREPRENEURS WHO HAD THE MOST PRODUCTIVE WORKERS. THE MOST PRODUCTIVE WORKERS WERE THOSE WHO WERE THE MOST CAPITALIZED OR IN OTHER WORDS THOSE WORKERS WHO UTILIZED THE MOST LABOR-SAVING INDUSTRIAL MACHINERY.

OF COURSE THINGS WERE NOT AS EASY AS ALL THAT. INDUSTRIALIZATION REQUIRED SAVING. AND AS ENGLAND'S EARLY INDUSTRIAL WORKERS DISCOVERED, THIS MEANT BEING PAID SUBSISTENCE WAGES.

TO KARL MARX, CAPITALISM WAS A DOOMED SOCIETY, DESTINED TO FAIL WHEN CAPITALISTS COULD NO LONGER EXTRACT PROFITS FROM DIMINISHING SURPLUS VALUE AS WORKERS BECAME MORE AND MORE CAPITALIZED. IN THE END HE PREDICTED THAT CAPITALISM, LIKE FEUDALISM BEFORE IT, WAS MERELY A TRANSITIONAL SOCIETY PAVING THE WAY FOR WHAT HE CALLED 'COMMUNISM.'

DESPITE MARX'S TELLING PREDICTIONS, CAPITALISM FLOURISHED AND SPREAD. IN AMERICA, CAPITALISM HAD THE ADDITIONAL ADVANTAGES OF BUILT-IN FRONTIERS AND AN EVER EXPANDING, NEARLY UNION-FREE, WORKFORCE. FURTHER, MOST AMERICANS SAW CAPITALISTS AS THE EPITOME OF WHAT AMERICA WAS ALL ABOUT.
REAL MEN ARE SELF-MADE MEN.
SO LONG AS TIMES WERE GOOD, AMERICA AND CAPITALISM WERE MADE TO ORDER FOR EACH OTHER.
U.S.A.
BUT WHEN THE BOOM YEARS OF THE 1920'S WENT BUST, CAPITALISM WAS IN FOR A CHANGE. NOT ONLY WAS THE DEPRESSION A DISASTROUS SETBACK FOR AMERICAN CAPITALISM, IT NEARLY RESULTED IN AN ABANDONMENT OF THE MARKET SYSTEM. THIS MIGHT HAVE HAPPENED HAD NOT JOHN MAYNARD KEYNES PROPOSED THE REMEDY OF GOVERNMENT INTERVENTION, A MOVE WHICH SAVED CAPITALISM AT THE COST OF REMOVING MORE THAN A FEW OF THE FEATURES OF THE OPEN MARKET. WE'LL MEET KEYNES AND HIS REMEDY IN THE NEXT CHAPTER.

PART 3
ESCAPE FROM THE OPEN MARKET

BY 1932 THE AMERICAN ECONOMY WAS IN A DEEP HOLE. PRESIDENT HOOVER MAINTAINED A 'HANDS OFF' APPROACH TO BUSINESS AND OFFERED AMERICANS POSITIVE WORDS FOR THE FUTURE. BUT 1932 WAS AN ELECTION YEAR AND AS HOOVER SOON REALIZED, AMERICANS WANTED GOVERNMENT TO ACT.

THE NEW DEAL

PRESIDENT ROOSEVELT WASTED LITTLE TIME IN GETTING THE BALL ROLLING. HE TOOK THE UNITED STATES OFF THE GOLD STANDARD SO THAT HIS DOMESTIC ECONOMIC POLICIES WOULD NOT BE ADVERSELY AFFECTED BY THE INTERNATIONAL FLOW OF GOLD IN AND OUT OF THE COUNTRY. THIS DONE, ROOSEVELT SOUGHT, AND USUALLY GOT, DRASTIC AND LONG-TERM CHANGES IN THE AMERICAN MARKET SYSTEM.

GUIDED CAPITALISM

IN THE BANKS

THE FIRST REFORMS OF NEW DEAL LEGISLATION DEALT MOSTLY WITH BANKING, PARTICULARLY WITH REGARD TO ITS INVOLVEMENT WITH THE STOCK MARKET. OF THE VARIOUS REFORMS, ONE OF THE MOST IMPORTANT ACTS WAS THE CREATION OF THE FEDERAL DEPOSITORS INSURANCE CORPORATION (F.D.I.C.). VEHEMENTLY OPPOSED BY THE NATION'S BANKERS AS AN INVITATION TO RECKLESSNESS, THE F.D.I.C. GUARANTEED THE SAFETY OF BANK DEPOSITS BY SIMPLY AND INEXPENSIVELY INSURING THEM, AND THE IDEA WORKED. THE F.D.I.C. NOT ONLY RESTORED PEOPLE'S FAITH IN THE BANKING INDUSTRY, IT SAVED QUITE A FEW BANKS. IN 1933, BEFORE THE F.D.I.C. WAS ENACTED, OVER 4,000 BANKS FAILED IN AMERICA. THE FOLLOWING YEAR, ONLY NINE INSURED BANKS FAILED, BUT THEIR DEPOSITORS WERE INSURED.

ON THE FARM

THE AGRICULTURAL ADJUSTMENT ACT WAS NEW DEAL LEGISLATION THAT REVOLUTIONIZED THE NATURE OF THE MARKET - TO THE FARMER'S ADVANTAGE. THE NEW DEAL FOR FARMERS RECOGNIZED THAT FARMERS FACE NEARLY PERFECT COMPETITION, THAT IS, NUMEROUS SELLERS ALL BIDDING THE PRICE DOWN, AND THAT DEMAND IS LIMITED, THAT IS, PEOPLE IN GOOD TIMES OR BAD CAN ONLY EAT SO MUCH FOOD. THEREFORE, IF YOU CAN'T INCREASE DEMAND... CUT BACK ON SUPPLY. THIS THE GOVERNMENT DID BY PAYING FARMERS, INITIALLY, TO DESTROY PORTIONS OF THEIR CROPS OR LIVESTOCK. THEN THE GOVERNMENT CONTINUED TO PAY FARMERS NOT TO PLANT CERTAIN CROPS OR TO LEAVE A CERTAIN PORTION OF LAND UNTILLED. THE RESULT? PRICES ON MOST FARM PRODUCTS DOUBLED, EVEN TRIPLED.

IN THE FACTORY

LABOR UNIONS, LIKE THE FEUDAL GUILDS WHICH PRECEDED THEM, WERE LONG THOUGHT TO BE THE VERY WORST THING TO HAVE HAPPEN TO AN OPEN MARKET. BUT DID THE OPEN MARKET EXIST ANYMORE ANYWAY? IN AN INTENSELY CAPITALIZED AND INDUSTRIALIZED MARKET SOCIETY, WHAT ADDITIONAL HARM COULD UNIONS BRING WHEN THEIR EMPLOYERS, MASSIVE CORPORATIONS, HAD ALREADY SUCCEEDED IN ELIMINATING ALL REAL COMPETITION. EVEN SO, THE STRUGGLE TO UNIONIZE WAS A BITTER ONE AND WITHOUT A SYMPATHETIC GOVERNMENT IN WASHINGTON, D.C., IT MIGHT NOT HAVE BEEN SUCCESSFUL.

POPULAR WITH FARMERS AND WORKERS, THE ROOSEVELT ADMINISTRATION AND AMERICAN BUSINESSMEN FOUND LITTLE IN COMMON OTHER THAN MUTUAL DISTRUST. AS FOR BUSINESSMEN, THEY WORRIED THAT ROOSEVELT WAS MOVING THE COUNTRY CLOSER TO SOCIALISM. TO ROOSEVELT, BUSINESSMEN WERE ALL TOO HYPOCRITICAL. THEY SEEMED TO LIKE THE IDEA OF LIMITING COMPETITION ONLY WHEN IT BENEFITTED THEM.

HOW WELL DID THE NEW DEAL WORK?

PROBLEMS PERSISTED. EVEN THOUGH FARMERS CUT BACK ON HOW MANY ACRES THEY FARMED, NEW TECHNOLOGY ENABLED THEM TO PRODUCE FAR MORE THAN THEY HAD EVER PRODUCED IN THE PAST. FOR WORKERS, EVEN THOUGH UNIONS WON WAGE CONCESSIONS AND BETTER WORKING CONDITIONS, FAR TOO MANY AMERICANS REMAINED OUT OF WORK. AS FOR BUSINESS, THEY SAW NO END TO THE DEPRESSION AND THEREFORE, NO REASON TO EXPAND. IT SEEMED HARD FOR MOST AMERICANS TO BELIEVE, BUT A FULL SIX YEARS HAD PASSED SINCE THE COLLAPSE OF THE STOCK MARKET AND, DESPITE THE BEST EFFORTS OF A CONCERNTED GOVERNMENT, VERY LITTLE HAD CHANGED.

UNDERSTANDING THE ROOT CAUSE OF...

THE DEPRESSION

WHILE THE CRASH PRECIPITATED THE DEPRESSION IT WAS NOT IN ITSELF RESPONSIBLE FOR ITS SEVERITY OR ITS DURATION. IT COULD BE SAID THAT THE DEPRESSION WAS CAUSED BY A FAILURE OF CONFIDENCE IN THE SYSTEM AND THAT WOULD BE TRUE. BUT, MORE ACCURATELY, THE DEPRESSION ENDURED BECAUSE OF A FAILURE IN A KEY MECHANISM OF CAPITALISM, THAT IS, THE RELATIONSHIP BETWEEN SAVINGS AND INVESTMENT.

IF YOU REMEMBER OUR DISCUSSION OF WHAT CAPITAL IS, YOU'LL RECALL THAT SOCIETIES MUST SAVE IN ORDER TO OBTAIN CAPITAL. NOT ONLY MUST SOCIETIES SAVE, THEY MUST INVEST IN A MARKET SOCIETY THOSE SAVINGS GO TOWARD PROFITABLE INVESTMENTS. BUT DURING THE DEPRESSION SAVINGS WERE HELD BACK. PROFITABLE INVESTMENTS WERE NOT THOUGHT POSSIBLE. THIS WAS A SELF-FULFILLING PROPHECY. AS FEWER CAPITAL GOODS (FACTORIES, MACHINERY) ARE PRODUCED, FEWER JOBS ARE CREATED. PRICES FALL, MORE JOBS ARE LOST. THIS DOWNWARD TREND CONTINUES UNTIL A SORT OF 'EQUILIBRIUM' IS ACHIEVED, ALBEIT ONE WELL BELOW A SOCIETY'S POTENTIAL. THE QUESTION, THEN, OF THE DAY WAS HOW TO RESTORE THE PROPER RELATIONSHIP BETWEEN SAVINGS AND INVESTMENT AND BRING ABOUT A DESIRED 'EQUILIBRIUM' OF FULL EMPLOYMENT AND FUTURE CAPITAL FORMATION.

JOHN MAYNARD KEYNES

1883
1946

IF CAPITALISM WAS FAILING, IT WAS KEYNES (CANES), MORE THAN ANYONE, WHO SOUGHT TO SAVE IT. KEYNES WAS AN ENGLISH ECONOMIST WHO STUDIED THE PROBLEM OF DEPRESSION AND PROPOSED WHAT WAS THEN CONSIDERED A RADICAL SOLUTION. IN HIS BOOK "THE GENERAL THEORY OF EMPLOYMENT, INTEREST AND MONEY," PUBLISHED IN 1936, KEYNES ARGUED THAT IT WAS POSSIBLE FOR A SOCIETY TO REMAIN INDEFINITELY AT AN EQUILIBRIUM BELOW POTENTIAL AND THAT THE SITUATION CALLED FOR GOVERNMENT INTERVENTION. THAT IS, THE GOVERNMENT SHOULD ENTER THE MARKETPLACE, MAKE MASS PURCHASES TO PROP UP DEMAND, & CREATE NEW JOBS AND RAISE OVERALL OUTPUT.

GOVERNMENT INTERVENTION IN THE MARKETPLACE WAS CALLED 'FISCAL POLICY' OR MORE AFFECTIONATELY KNOWN AS...

FOR OTHERS IT WAS SOMETHING FAR WORSE THAN THAT...

BUT WHAT ELSE WAS THERE TO DO? MONETARY POLICY, WHICH THE FED WAS RESPONSIBLE FOR, DIDN'T SEEM TO HAVE THE ANSWERS. SO MAYBE IT WAS TIME FOR SOMETHING NEW. AFTER ALL, THE 1930'S MAY HAVE BEEN HARD TIMES FOR AMERICANS, BUT THEY WERE, SPEAKING STRICTLY ECONOMICALLY, ROBUST FOR NAZI GERMANY AND THE SOVIET UNION, TWO COUNTRIES THAT, WHETHER THEY KNEW IT OR NOT, WERE BIG ON FISCAL POLICY. AND FROM AN ECONOMIST'S SEAT NEITHER COUNTRY HAD ANY PROBLEM WITH UNEMPLOYMENT.

POLICY DEBATE
FISCAL ·VS· MONETARY
TO REDUCE UNEMPLOYMENT, THE GOVERNMENT MUST STEP IN AND CREATE JOBS.
MISTAKE! BUSINESS WANTS TO EXPAND. JUST LOWER THE DISCOUNT RATE TO THE POINT WHERE BUSINESS WILL BORROW.
BUSINESS MAY NEVER WANT TO BORROW. GOVERNMENT MUST BE THE ONE TO BORROW AND STIMULATE DEMAND.
STIMULATE INFLATION YOU MEAN. BETTER TO ALLOW FOR SLOW, STEADY GROWTH IN THE MONEY SUPPLY. JUST ENOUGH TO MEET THE NEEDS OF A GROWING ECONOMY.
WHAT GROWING ECONOMY? IT WON'T GROW UNTIL PRICES ARE RESTORED...
INFLATION!
ALL RIGHT, INFLATION. BUT IT'S PREFERABLE TO UNEMPLOYMENT. BESIDES, GOVERNMENT CAN CHECK INFLATION BY RAISING TAXES.
HIGHER TAXES! THAT WOULD ONLY REDUCE INCENTIVE. ALL THIS ECONOMY NEEDS IS SLOW, STEADY GROWTH.
GOVERNMENT INTERVENTION
PRIVATE INDUSTRY.
STARVE A COLD, FEED A FEVER.
FEED A COLD, STARVE A FEVER.
FISCAL
MONETARY

THE LAST GASP of the FED

WITH THE F.D.I.C. IN PLACE AND CONFIDENCE SOMEWHAT RESTORED IN THE BANKING SYSTEM. BANK DEPOSITS BEGAN TO BUILD UP. THAT IS, PEOPLE WERE NOW WILLING TO DEPOSIT WHAT SAVINGS THEY HAD INTO BANKS. BUT VERY FEW PEOPLE WERE WILLING TO COME INTO BANKS TO BORROW THAT MONEY. AND THAT, SAID THE FED, WAS A POTENTIALLY DISASTROUS SITUATION.

EVEN THOUGH SUCH AN OCCURRENCE MIGHT SEEM A BLESSING TO MANY, THE FED SAW SUCH A SITUATION AS ONE NEEDING CORRECTION, AND SO THE FED RAISED THE RESERVE REQUIREMENT THIS ACTION EFFECTIVELY CUT OFF WHAT LITTLE RECOVERY WAS TAKING PLACE IN THE ECONOMY AT THE TIME AND WAS AT LEAST PARTIALLY RESPONSIBLE FOR SETTING OFF A SORT OF RECESSION WITHIN A DEPRESSION. FOR THIS REASON, AND ITS PAST RECORD, IT WOULD BE ANOTHER GENERATION BEFORE ANYONE BOTHERED MUCH WITH THE FED AND ITS USE OF MONETARY POLICY.

THE FISCAL CURE

FOR KEYNESIAN ECONOMICS AND FISCAL POLICY TO PROVE ITSELF THE GOVERNMENT WOULD HAVE TO MAKE MASSIVE PURCHASES TO DO THIS, THE GOVERNMENT WOULD HAVE TO BE WILLING TO SPEND MORE, MUCH MORE, THAN IT TOOK IN THIS WAS NOT AN EASY THING FOR MOST AMERICANS TO ACCEPT. NOT EVEN FOR ROOSEVELT.

"ANY GOVERNMENT, LIKE ANY FAMILY, CAN FOR A YEAR SPEND A LITTLE MORE THAN IT EARNS. BUT YOU AND I KNOW THAT A CONTINUATION OF THAT HABIT MEANS THE POORHOUSE."

THESE WERE NOT THE WORDS OF A CONSERVATIVE BUSINESSMAN, THIS WAS THE NATION'S LEADING LIBERAL SPEAKING. AND SO IT SEEMED THAT, AS THE 1930'S CAME TO END, IF THE GOVERNMENT WERE TO STEP IN AND SPEND ITSELF OUT OF THE DEPRESSION SOMETHING MORE DIRE THAN MERE HIGH UNEMPLOYMENT WOULD HAVE TO PROD IT. BY 1940, THAT PROD WAS NOT LONG IN COMING.

WORLD WAR II

THE MASSIVE GOVERNMENT EXPENDITURES WHICH THE WAR CALLED FOR AND THE SUBSEQUENT DROP IN THE UNEMPLOYMENT RATE AFFIRMED, ONCE AND FOR ALL THE WISDOM OF KEYNESIAN ECONOMICS. THAT IS, A GOVERNMENT COULD UTILIZE FISCAL POLICY TO SPEND ITSELF OUT OF A DEPRESSION.

BUT WHAT ABOUT INFLATION?

ONE OF THE PERSISTANT PROBLEMS OF A NATION AT WAR IS INFLATION. AS THE WORK FORCE DECLINES, WAGES TEND TO GO UP. THIS IS A SERIOUS PROBLEM IN A MARKET ECONOMY BECAUSE RISING MILITARY PURCHASES MUST NOT BE THREATENED BY RISING CONSUMER PURCHASES. DURING W.W. II GOVERNMENT DID PRACTICALLY EVERYTHING TO PREVENT NONMILITARY CONSUMPTION.

TAXES	TAXES WERE RAISED THOUGHOUT THE WAR. BUT NOT NEARLY ENOUGH TO PAY THE ENORMOUS COSTS.
GOVT. BONDS	THE GOVERNMENT SOLD BONDS TO THE PUBLIC BOTH TO RAISE MONEY AND TO DEPRIVE THE PUBLIC OF MONEY THEY MIGHT OTHERWISE SPEND DURING THE WAR.
RATIONING	FOR CERTAIN ESSENTIAL ITEMS LIKE GASOLINE, THE GOVERNMENT ISSUED RATION COUPONS. THIS PERMITTED THE GOVERNMENT CONTROL OVER CONSUMER DEMAND.

BUT THE AMERICAN GOVERNMENT WENT EVEN ONE STEP FURTHER.

WAGE & PRICE CONTROLS

AS A FINAL ASSAULT ON THE THREAT OF INFLATION THE AMERICAN GOVERNMENT IMPOSED STIFF WAGE AND PRICE CONTROLS ON PRACTICALLY EVERYTHING, UP UNTIL THE WAR'S END. DID THE CONTROLS WORK? YES, PRICES REMAINED STABLE, BUT OF GREATER IMPORTANCE WAS THE FACT THAT THE AMERICAN GOVERNMENT, BY DESIGN, NO LONGER OVERSAW A MARKET ECONOMY. THE GOVERNMENT, NOT THE MARKET, DETERMINED THE LEVEL OF WAGES AND PRICES. IT WAS THE GOVERNMENT, NOT CONSUMER DEMAND, THAT DETERMINED WHAT PRODUCTS WOULD BE PROVIDED, AND IN SOME CASES DISTRIBUTION (WHO GOT HOW MUCH) WAS NO LONGER DETERMINED BY MONEY BUT BY GOVERNMENT RATION COUPONS.

WHILE THE AMERICAN GOVERNMENT HAD EXPERIMENTED WITH PRICE CONTROLS BEFORE, IT WAS NEVER AS PERVASIVE AS DURING WORLD WAR II. AND IT MADE ONE THING VERY CLEAR. THE GOVERNMENT KNEW, AND SO DID EVERYONE ELSE, THAT IT NOW HAD THE TOOLS AND THE POWER AND THE WILL TO ALTER MARKET CONDITIONS. THIS MEANT THAT THE DAYS OF HANDS-OFF GOVERNMENT WERE OVER. FROM NOW ON THE VOTING PUBLIC COULD HOLD THE POLITICIANS RESPONSIBLE FOR THE ECONOMIC PERFORMANCE OF THE COUNTRY. TO DO THIS EFFECTIVELY, ECONOMISTS HAD TO DEVISE GUIDES OR STANDARDS TO MEASURE PERFORMANCE.

GROSS NATIONAL PRODUCT
"WHAT'S SO DISGUSTING ABOUT IT?"
G.N.P. IS ONE SUCH GUIDE FOR TRACKING ECONOMIC PERFORMANCE. G.N.P. IS THE GRAND SUM TOTAL OF ALL FINISHED GOODS AND SERVICES PURCHASED BY CONSUMERS, BUSINESSES AND GOVERNMENT.
"FINISHED GOODS? WANNA' EXPLAIN THAT!"
A LOAF OF BREAD IS A FINISHED GOOD. ITS SALE PRICE REFLECTS PRIOR SALES WHICH ARE NOT INCLUDED IN G.N.P. THAT IS, THE SALE OF WHEAT FROM A FARMER TO A MILLER, THE SALE OF FLOUR FROM A MILLER TO A BAKER, THE SALE OF BREAD FROM A BAKER TO A GROCER ARE ALL PRIOR SALES. ONLY THE FINAL SALE OF THE FINISHED GOOD, FROM THE GROCER TO THE CUSTOMER, IS IN G.N.P.
"WHAT ABOUT IMPORTS AND EXPORTS?"
EXPORT SALES ARE ADDED BUT IMPORTS ARE SUBTRACTED.
"SO YOU ADD IT ALL UP AND G.N.P. IS WHAT YOU GET. WHAT ABOUT PER CAPITA G.N.P.? WHAT'S THAT?
"ONE PER CAPITA, TWO PER CAPITA, THREE PER CAPITA, FOUR."
SIMPLE. PER CAPITA'S ARE PEOPLE. JUST TAKE THE NUMBER OF PEOPLE IN A COUNTRY, DIVIDE THE NUMBER INTO G.N.P. AND 'VOILA' ~ 'PER CAPITA G.N.P.'

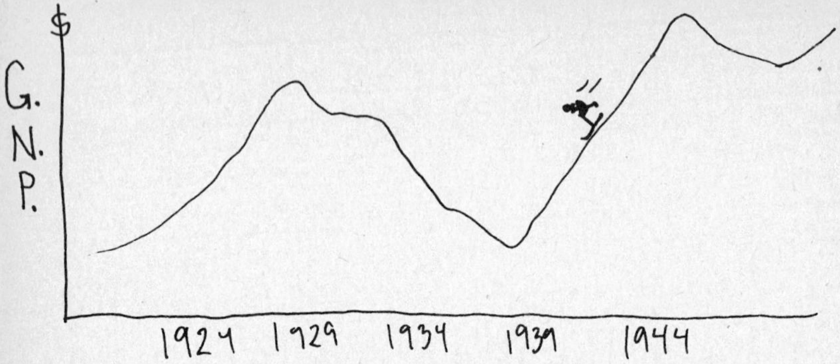

G.N.P. CAN BE MISLEADING...

...BECAUSE OF INFLATION. THAT IS, IF INFLATION SENDS PRICES HIGHER, THEN G.N.P. WILL APPEAR TO HAVE GONE UP. BUT IN REALITY GOODS PRODUCED AND SOLD MIGHT ACTUALLY HAVE FALLEN.

PRICE INDEX

A PRICE INDEX IS A STANDARD WHICH ALLOWS ECONOMISTS TO MEASURE WHAT AMOUNT OF INCREASE IN THE G.N.P. CAN BE ATTRIBUTED TO INFLATION.

CONSUMER PRICE INDEX

MUCH LIKE THE G.N.P., THE C.P.I. IS A COMMONLY USED GAUGE TO MEASURE AN ECONOMY'S PERFORMANCE. AS WITH ANY OTHER PRICE INDEX THE C.P.I. MEASURES INFLATION. BUT AS THE NAME IMPLIES IT PAYS PARTICULAR ATTENTION TO THE PRICES OF CONSUMER GOODS.

1948-1968 GOOD TIMES

IF YOU'LL RECALL, DURING THE DEPRESSION FEW BUSINESSES BORROWED AND INVESTED MONEY INTO CAPITAL BECAUSE THE POTENTIAL FOR PROFIT SEEMED BLEAK. HOWEVER W.W. II CHANGED THAT THINKING. FIRST THERE WAS MUCH REBUILDING OF EUROPE AND JAPAN TO BE DONE. SECONDLY, SINCE THE GOVERNMENT CURTAILED CONSUMER DEMAND DURING THE WAR, CONSUMER SPENDING AFTER THE WAR WAS SURE TO BE STRONG. FINALLY, IT APPEARED THAT GOVERNMENT MILITARY INVESTMENT WOULD CONTINUE RATHER THAN SUDDENLY STOP.

BUT AN ONGOING MILITARY BUILDUP WAS NOT THE ONLY WAY THAT THE AMERICAN GOVERNMENT PLANNED TO KEEP ONE FOOT IN THE MARKET. CONGRESS ALSO PASSED THE EMPLOYMENT ACT OF 1946. THE EMPLOYMENT ACT SAW TO IT THAT GOVERNMENT WOULD HAVE AN ONGOING ROLE IN ASSURING THAT PEOPLE STAYED OUT OF THE UNEMPLOYMENT LINES.
"WELL, NO WONDER I NEEDED SUCH A TALL HAT!"
"THE FIRST THING GOVERNMENT SHOULD DO TO REDUCE UNEMPLOYMENT, IS HIRE LOTS OF ECONOMISTS!"
AS IT TURNED OUT THE 1950's AND 60's WERE GOOD TIMES FOR MOST PEOPLE, PARTICULARLY GOVERNMENT ECONOMISTS. PRICES WERE FAIRLY STABLE, G.N.P. WAS ON AN UPWARD TREND, THE DOLLAR WAS BACK ON THE GOLD STANDARD, AND FISCAL POLICY PROVED A RELIABLE TOOL FOR PUMPING UP THE ECONOMY.
O.K., SURE... MR. FISCAL 'GOT ALL THE ANSWERS' POLICY, YOU CAN DEAL WITH DEPRESSION AND UNEMPLOYMENT. BUT I WANT TO KNOW HOW YOU'RE GOING TO DEAL WITH INFLATION... HMM?
WELL... I...
MR FISCAL
MR. MONETARY

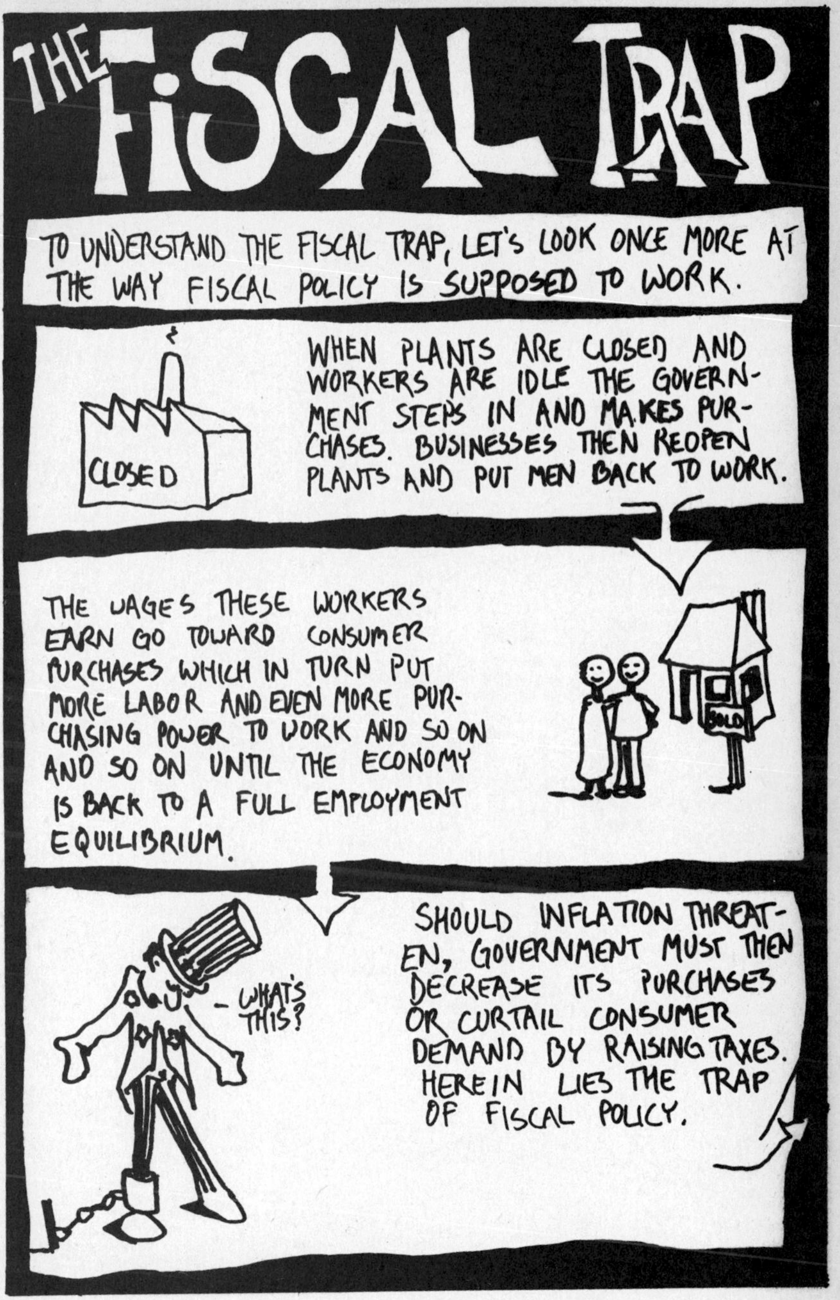
THE FISCAL TRAP
TO UNDERSTAND THE FISCAL TRAP, LET'S LOOK ONCE MORE AT THE WAY FISCAL POLICY IS SUPPOSED TO WORK.
CLOSED
WHEN PLANTS ARE CLOSED AND WORKERS ARE IDLE THE GOVERNMENT STEPS IN AND MAKES PURCHASES. BUSINESSES THEN REOPEN PLANTS AND PUT MEN BACK TO WORK.
THE WAGES THESE WORKERS EARN GO TOWARD CONSUMER PURCHASES WHICH IN TURN PUT MORE LABOR AND EVEN MORE PURCHASING POWER TO WORK AND SO ON AND SO ON UNTIL THE ECONOMY IS BACK TO A FULL EMPLOYMENT EQUILIBRIUM.
SOLD
– WHAT'S THIS?
SHOULD INFLATION THREATEN, GOVERNMENT MUST THEN DECREASE ITS PURCHASES OR CURTAIL CONSUMER DEMAND BY RAISING TAXES. HEREIN LIES THE TRAP OF FISCAL POLICY.

END THE F111B PROJECT? BUT YOU'LL THROW HUNDREDS OUT OF WORK!
YOU CAN'T END FARM SUBSIDIES!
RAISE TAXES?! RAISE TAXES?! YOU'RE CRAZY!
WHAT HAVE I GOT MYSELF INTO?
IN A DEMOCRATIC SOCIETY, POLITICAL PRESSURE ENSURES THAT FISCAL POLICY HAS FIVE GEARS FORWARD BUT NONE FOR REVERSE.
HA! I LOVE IT. THE FISCAL TRAP AND YOU WALKED HEADLONG INTO IT. YOU THOUGHT YOU COULD DO EVERYTHING... CREATE A WELFARE STATE, CONTAIN COMMUNISM IN INDO-CHINA... GIVE EVERYONE WHATEVER THEY WANTED. **BUT** WHEN IT CAME TIME TO ADJUST FOR INFLATION BY CUTTING BACK ON EXPENDITURES OR RAISING TAXES YOU COULDN'T DO IT! NOW LOOK AT THE MESS WE'RE IN!
MR FISCAL
MR. MONETARY

BY 1968 THE AMERICAN ECONOMY WAS CLEARLY HEADED FOR TROUBLE. ALTHOUGH A SURTAX WAS LEVIED THAT YEAR TO HELP PAY THE COSTS OF THE VIETNAM WAR, IT WAS THE FIRST SUCH TAX AND ONLY A TEMPORARY ONE AT THAT. FURTHER, THE WAR WAS ESCALATING AND BECOMING LESS POPULAR; THE PROSPECTS FOR LEVYING OTHER TAXES WERE NOT GOOD. MEANWHILE AT HOME, POWERFUL UNIONS WERE DEMANDING AND GETTING MAJOR WAGE GAINS WHILE POWERFUL CORPORATIONS, WITH LITTLE FEAR OF COMPETITION, WERE EASILY MARKING UP PRICES. SO WHERE WERE THE SOLUTIONS IF NOT WITH FISCAL POLICY? MILTON FRIEDMAN, AN ECONOMIST FROM THE U. of CHICAGO, SOUGHT TO POPULARIZE 'MONETARY POLICY' ONCE AGAIN. THAT IS, DECREASE PRICES BY RAISING INTEREST RATES, THEREBY SLACKENING THE DESIRE OF BUSINESSES TO BORROW MONEY, WHICH WOULD ACT TO HALT EXPANSION, HIRING AND EVENTUALLY SLOW DOWN THE ENTIRE ECONOMY.

BUT WHY WOULD ANYONE WANT TO PICK UP THE TORCH OF MONETARY POLICY? AFTER ALL, IT WAS THE FED'S FAILURE TO ADMINISTER MONETARY POLICY CORRECTLY WHICH FUELED THE STOCK MARKET BOOM AND WORSENED THE DEPRESSION.
I DON'T DENY IT. IT WAS THE FAILURE OF THE FED, NOT MONETARY POLICY. IF MONETARY POLICY HAD BEEN USED TO GRADUALLY, SLOWLY AND STEADILY INCREASE THE MONEY SUPPLY NEITHER THE BOOM NOR THE DEPRESSION NEED HAVE OCCURRED.
MILT.
FRIEDMAN STAUNCHLY OPPOSED FISCAL POLICY. AS HE SAW IT, EVERYTHING GOOD STEMMED FROM THE UNTARNISHED SANCTITY OF THE OPEN MARKET. PROSPERITY, PERSONAL FREEDOM, FULL EMPLOYMENT AND STABLE PRICES; THESE THINGS CAME ABOUT WHERE THERE WERE NO BARRIERS TO COMPETITION AND NO ROOM FOR GOVERNMENT INTERVENTION.
IT'S SIMPLE... YOU CHOKE OFF THE MONEY SUPPLY THRU HIGHER INTEREST RATES. BUSINESSES WILL CEASE TO EXPAND, FEWER JOBS WILL BE CREATED AND PRICES WILL STABILIZE...
YOU MEAN THROW A LOT OF WORKERS OUT OF WORK.
TEMPORARILY, BUT THE EFFECT WOULD BE NO WORSE THAN IF YOU COULD RAISE TAXES OR ELIMINATE GOVERNMENT SPENDING, BUT WE BOTH KNOW YOU CAN'T DO THAT!
YOUR WAY IS WORSE.
AT LEAST IT CAN DE DONE.
MR FISCAL
MR MONETARY

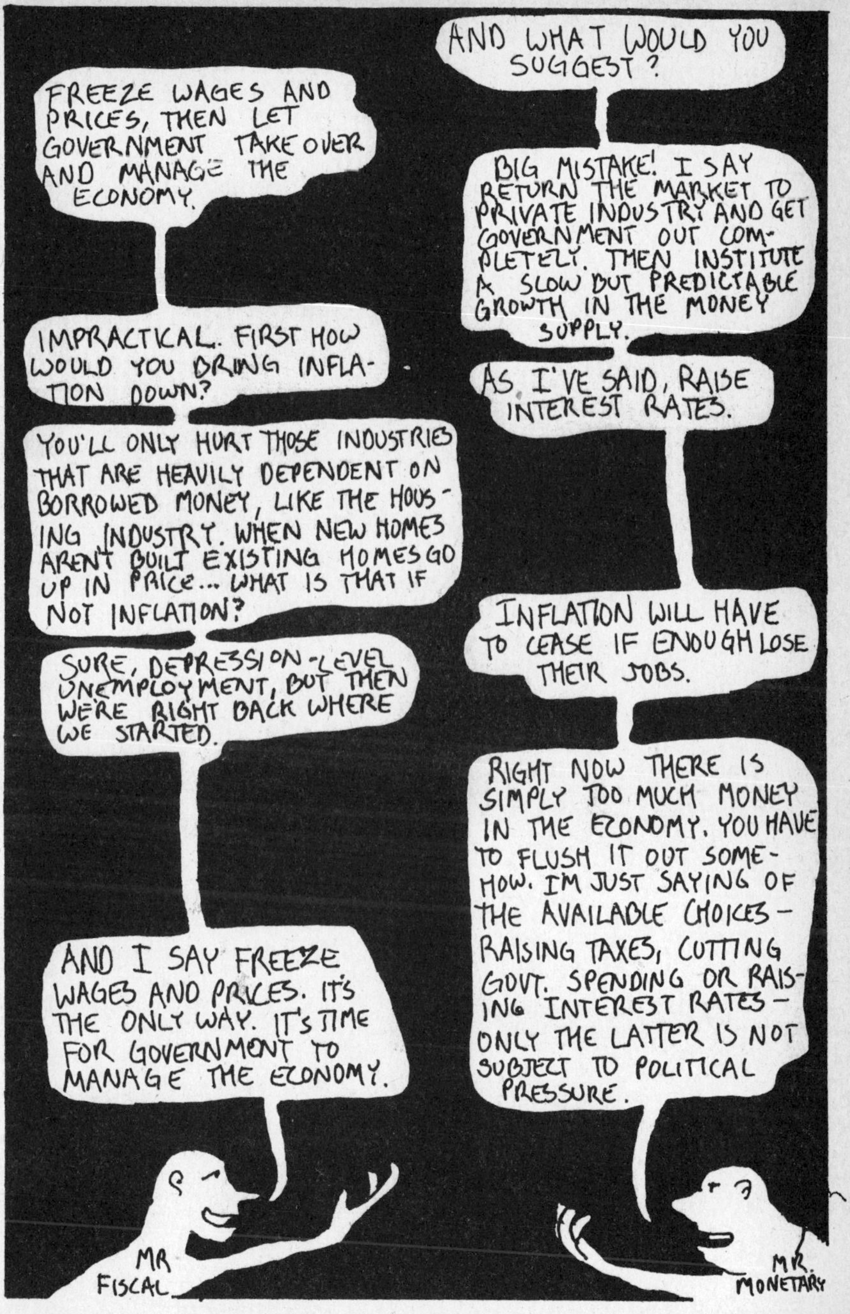
AND WHAT WOULD YOU SUGGEST?
FREEZE WAGES AND PRICES, THEN LET GOVERNMENT TAKE OVER AND MANAGE THE ECONOMY.
BIG MISTAKE! I SAY RETURN THE MARKET TO PRIVATE INDUSTRY AND GET GOVERNMENT OUT COMPLETELY. THEN INSTITUTE A SLOW BUT PREDICTABLE GROWTH IN THE MONEY SUPPLY.
IMPRACTICAL. FIRST HOW WOULD YOU BRING INFLATION DOWN?
AS I'VE SAID, RAISE INTEREST RATES.
YOU'LL ONLY HURT THOSE INDUSTRIES THAT ARE HEAVILY DEPENDENT ON BORROWED MONEY, LIKE THE HOUSING INDUSTRY. WHEN NEW HOMES AREN'T BUILT EXISTING HOMES GO UP IN PRICE... WHAT IS THAT IF NOT INFLATION?
INFLATION WILL HAVE TO CEASE IF ENOUGH LOSE THEIR JOBS.
SURE, DEPRESSION-LEVEL UNEMPLOYMENT, BUT THEN WE'RE RIGHT BACK WHERE WE STARTED.
RIGHT NOW THERE IS SIMPLY TOO MUCH MONEY IN THE ECONOMY. YOU HAVE TO FLUSH IT OUT SOMEHOW. I'M JUST SAYING OF THE AVAILABLE CHOICES—RAISING TAXES, CUTTING GOVT. SPENDING OR RAISING INTEREST RATES—ONLY THE LATTER IS NOT SUBJECT TO POLITICAL PRESSURE.
AND I SAY FREEZE WAGES AND PRICES. IT'S THE ONLY WAY. IT'S TIME FOR GOVERNMENT TO MANAGE THE ECONOMY.
MR FISCAL
MR. MONETARY

FROM 1968 TO 1974 JUST ABOUT EVERYTHING WAS TRIED. INTEREST RATES WERE RAISED, A TEMPORARY SURTAX WAS LEVIED, THE DOLLAR WAS TAKEN OFF THE GOLD STANDARD AND FINALLY IN 1973 PRESIDENT NIXON FROZE WAGES AND PRICES. BUT THE FREEZE LASTED ONLY LONG ENOUGH TO STABILIZE PRICES AND REELECT NIXON TO A SECOND TERM. WHEN THE FREEZE WAS LIFTED IN JANUARY OF 1973 BOTH INFLATION AND UNEMPLOYMENT WENT UP AGAIN.

BUT THEN IN 1974 THESE ARGUMENTS BECAME SOMEWHAT ACADEMIC.

THE ARAB OIL EMBARGO AND THE RESULTANT INCREASE IN THE PRICE OF OIL HAD THE EFFECT OF A HUGE SALES TAX. THAT IS, IT FLUSHED BILLIONS OF DOLLARS OUT OF THE AMERICAN MARKETPLACE. THEREFORE, ITS INITIAL IMPACT, RATHER THAN BEING INFLATIONARY, ACTUALLY SOFTENED DEMAND FOR OTHER CONSUMER GOODS. HOWEVER, NEW FEARS OF INFLATION WERE AROUSED WHEN MUCH OF THE MONEY CAME BACK AS DEPOSITS INTO AMERICAN BANKS. SHOULD THIS NEWLY DEPOSITED MONEY, ALONG WITH THE VAST NEW SUMS CREATED FROM IT, GO OUT INTO THE MARKET, THE POTENTIAL FOR INFLATION-OUT-OF-CONTROL WOULD BE ENORMOUS.

THIS POSSIBILITY WAS SOMEWHAT CHECKED BY THE FED. USING MONETARY POLICY, THE FED BOOSTED THE DISCOUNT RATE TO UNHEARD-OF HIGH LEVELS. BUT IT SEEMED TOO LITTLE, TOO LATE. AMERICANS HAD ALREADY DEVELOPED AN INFLATION PSYCHOLOGY. THAT IS, BUY NOW, EVEN WITH BORROWED MONEY, BECAUSE THE PRICES OF GOODS WILL SURELY BE HIGHER COME TOMORROW.

BY THE LATE 1970'S THE SITUATION WAS BAD AND ONLY GETTING WORSE. SINCE PASSBOOK SAVINGS ACCOUNTS COULD NOT, BY LAW, PAY MORE THAN 5¼%, AMERICANS SOUGHT INVESTMENTS THAT COULD AT LEAST KEEP PACE WITH INFLATION. FOR MOST AMERICANS THIS MEANT LAND AND HOUSING. LAND, AS DAVID RICARDO POINTED OUT OVER A HUNDRED AND FIFTY YEARS EARLIER, WAS FINITE AND COULD NOT, UNLIKE MONEY, BE CREATED. AND HOUSING, SO LONG AS INTEREST RATES REMAINED PROHIBITIVELY HIGH, WAS ALSO REGARDED AS A GOOD PLACE TO INVEST MONEY.

UNFORTUNATELY, DEMAND FOR LAND AND HOUSING REACHED A SPECULATIVE PITCH, WHICH BECAME DEPENDENT ON AN EVER SURGING RATE OF INFLATION.

INFLATION BECAME A NECESSARY EVIL FOR GOVERNMENT AS WELL. HERE'S HOW...
"BOSS, YOU GOTTA GIVE ME A RAISE JUST SO I CAN KEEP PACE WITH INFLATION."
HIGHER INCOMES MEANT HIGHER PRICES WHICH REQUIRED HIGHER INCOMES, JUST TO KEEP BUYING POWER CONSTANT.
WHILE HIGHER INCOME MAY NOT HAVE INCREASED BUYING POWER IT CERTAINLY PUSHED PEOPLE INTO HIGHER TAX BRACKETS. THIS PLAYED INTO THE HANDS OF GOVERNMENT SINCE IT RESULTED IN INCREASED TAX REVENUES WITHOUT LEVYING NEW TAXES.
END TAXATION BY INFLATION
I PAY PETER YOU PAY PAUL.
UNFORTUNATELY GOVERNMENT FOUND THAT INCREASED REVENUES MERELY OFFSET INCREASED EXPENDITURES SINCE GOVERNMENT HANDOUTS WERE ALWAYS ADJUSTED UPWARD TO OFFSET INFLATION.
ANY EXCESS REVENUES WERE NEEDED TO HELP PAY OFF THE NATIONAL DEBT WHICH WAS GETTING WORSE DUE TO HIGHER INTEREST RATES.
IS IT POSSIBLE THAT YOU'RE GETTING OUT OF HAND?
DEBT

AS WE MENTIONED EARLIER, AMERICANS WERE SPENDING MONEY. UNFORTUNATELY, MOST OF THESE SALES WERE GOING TO FOREIGN-MADE GOODS. THIS NOT ONLY HURT AMERICAN G.N.P. IT SHARPLY WEAKENED AMERICAN CORPORATE POWER. THAT IS, MANY AMERICAN CORPORATIONS (EX. CHRYSLER) WERE UNPREPARED TO FACE A SITUATION THAT THEY HAD LONG THOUGHT WAS AN OLD FORGOTTEN MEMORY.

IT WAS NO ACCIDENT EITHER THAT MOST OF THE FOREIGN COMPETITION CAME FROM GERMANY AND JAPAN, TWO NATIONS WHOSE PRODUCTIVE POWERS HAD BEEN DESTROYED DURING WORLD WAR II, THEN REBUILT WITH AMERICAN AID. THIS REBUILDING UTILIZED THE MOST RECENT TECHNOLOGY AVAILABLE AND AS SUCH IT RENDERED AMERICAN PRODUCTIVE POWER COMPARATIVELY OBSOLETE, **AND** AMERICAN LABOR COMPARATIVELY UNDERCAPITALIZED, OR IN OTHER WORDS, LESS PRODUCTIVE. IN PRACTICAL TERMS, THIS MEANT THAT LABOR UNIONS WERE SEEKING AND GETTING WAGE GAINS IN EXCESS OF PRODUCTIVITY GAINS AND AMERICAN CORPORATIONS WERE MAINTAINING PROFIT MARGINS THROUGH COST CUTTING. THIS WAS A SITUATION THAT COULD ONLY GO ON SO LONG.

WELL HERE WE ARE, 1979, FIFTY YEARS AFTER THE GREAT STOCK MARKET CRASH, AND I WONDER, ARE WE ANY BETTER OFF?
I THINK WE'RE WORSE OFF. NOT ONLY IS THERE RECORD UN-EMPLOYMENT THERE'S RUNAWAY INFLATION AS WELL. AND IT'S ALL BECAUSE OF FISCAL POLICY.
SURE, BLAME FISCAL POLICY FOR INFLATION, BUT IT'S MONE-TARY POLICY THAT CAUSED SUCH HIGH UNEMPLOYMENT.
WELL WHATEVER, THE POINT IS WE'VE GOT TO FIND A WAY OUT OF THIS MESS.
AS I'VE SAID BEFORE... LET THE GOVERNMENT PLAN THE ECONOMY. SET WAGES AND PRICES AND NATIONALIZE MAJOR CORPORATIONS. THEN EXTEND SOCIAL PROGRAMS.
BUT THAT WOULD MAKE US INTO VIRTUALLY A COMMUNIST COUNTRY.
WELL IF IT ALLEVIATES TENSION BETWEN THE U.S. AND RUSSIA I SAY ALL THE BETTER. BESIDES, WHAT ALTERNATIVE IS THERE?
OH, I DONT KNOW, MAYBE SOME HERO FIGURE COULD COME ALONG, CUT FEDERAL SPENDING AND REMAIN POPULAR ENOUGH TO BE REELECTED.
NOW YOU'RE TALKING HOLLYWOOD, NOT AMERICAN POLITICS.
YES I SUPPOSE YOU'RE RIGHT.
MR FISCAL
MR. MONETARY.

THE CONTINUING SAGA OF THE BOX COMPANY
PART II
THE BOX SAGA CONTINUES AND CONCLUDES WITH A LOOK AT HOW THIS NEARLY FACTUAL MOSTLY FICTIONAL AMERICAN CORPORATION WINDS ITS WAY THROUGH THE TWENTIETH CENTURY.
JOHN BLOCK
OLD, INFIRM AND REPORTEDLY RABID, JOHN BLOCK (MUCH TO OGILVY'S DISMAY) NEVER QUITE DRIFTED INTO OBSCURITY. IN 1920, WHEN BLOCK WAS IN HIS 80'S, HE MADE A SUCCESSFUL BID FOR CONGRESS. THOUGH HE DIED WITHIN A WEEK OF BEING SEATED HE WILL ALWAYS BE REMEMBERED AS THE CONGRESSMAN WHO WRESTLED PRESIDENT HARDING AND PINNED HIM DOWN ONTO THE WHITEHOUSE LAWN
MORRIS OGILVY III
SHORTLY AFTER HIS GRANDFATHER CAUGHT A LOAD OF BRICKS (ANARCHISTS WERE SUSPECTED BUT NEVER CHARGED) DURING AN OVERSEAS PLANT INSPECTION, YOUNG MORRIS THE THIRD WAS NAMED SUCCESSOR TO THE CHAIRMANSHIP OF BOX INTERNATIONAL. GENEROUSLY DESCRIBED AS INCOMPETENT, YOUNG MORRIS WASTED LITTLE TIME IN REDUCING THE ASKING PRICE FOR BOX-STOCK THREEFOLD
BOB HAYES
TAKING THE HELM OF BOX IN 1936 HAYES CAME TO REPRESENT THE EPITOME OF A NEW STYLE OF AMERICAN BUSINESSMAN. HE WAS BRASH AND RUTHLESS BUT HE NEVER OWNED EVEN ONE SHARE OF BOX STOCK, AND YET HE GUIDED BOX INTO THE TWENTIETH CENTURY AND INTO THE ELITE CLASSIFICATION OF AMERICAN CORPORATIONS KNOWN AS 'BLUE CHIP.'

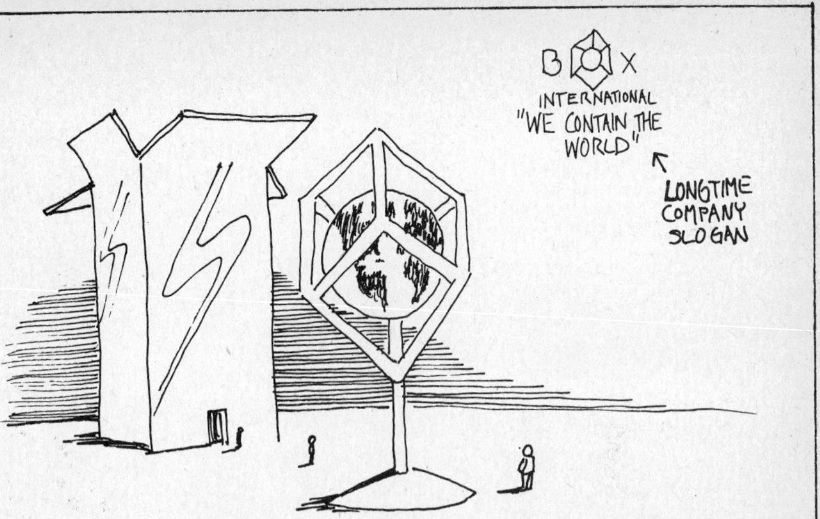

THE WHIMSICALLY DESIGNED (BUILT UNDER THE DIRECTION OF MORRIS III) CORPORATE HEADQUARTERS OF BOX INTERNATIONAL. IN THE FOREGROUND IS THE SIXTY-FOOT-HIGH SYMBOL OF BOX'S LOGO.

1941 THE WAR YEARS 1945

WHEN CONSUMER DEMAND FELL OFF DURING THE WAR YEARS, BOX'S CONSUMER PACKAGING DIVISION FELL INTO A SERIOUS SALES SLUMP. EVEN THOUGH MILITARY SHELL & CASING ORDERS MORE THAN COVERED ANY POTENTIAL OVERALL LOSS FROM THE CONSUMER DIVISION, CHAIRMAN HAYES LAID OUT A BRILLIANT PROMOTION WHICH UTILIZED POPULAR COMIC STRIP CHARACTERS 'PALOOKA PAT AND MOLLY.' THE PROMOTION NOT ONLY KEPT THE CONSUMER PACKAGING DIVISION AT FULL PRODUCTION IT BROUGHT IN TONS OF SCRAP METAL FOR VIRTUALLY NOTHING.

1948 THE GLORY YEARS 1965

REAR ADMIRAL
PRESTON WEBB
CHAIRMAN OF BOX INDUSTRIES
1952-1967

EVER SINCE THE CIVIL WAR DAYS BOX HAS MAINTAINED A STRONG TRADITION OF COMING TO THE NATION'S DEFENSE. THIS TRADITION WAS NEVER MORE HONORED THAN WITH THE ANNOUNCEMENT THAT REAR ADMIRAL PRESTON WEBB WOULD SUCCEED BOB HAYES AS CHAIRMAN OF THE BOARD OF BOX INDUSTRIES. WEBB'S ASCENSION TO THE THRONE COULD NOT HAVE BEEN MORE FORTUNATE FOR BOX'S PROFITABILITY. THE 50'S WERE YEARS OF MILITARY MUSCLE FLEXING AND NONE COULD DOUBT THAT IT WAS WEBB'S CLOSE TIES TO PROCURERS WITH THE PENTAGON THAT BROUGHT BOX UNPRECEDENTED DEFENSE CONTRACTS. SO PROFITABLE WERE THE DEFENSE CONTRACTS THAT BOX SOON WENT ON A CORPORATE SHOPPING SPREE, MAKING SUCH DIVERSE ACQUISITIONS AS MRS. HOPE'S KITCHENS (SNACK FOODS) AND KARL WALLENDA GYM SETS (PLAYGROUND EQUIPMENT). AND TO PROMOTE THEIR NEW FORAYS INTO CONSUMER GOODS, BOX PRODUCED ONE OF THE LONGEST RUNNING TELEVISION SERIES, THE BOX FAMILY THEATRE.

THEN CAME DISASTER

THE BOOK:

THE AUTHOR: CONSUMER ADVOCATE CHARLES PROESSOR.

DISASTER STRUCK FIRST WITH THE PUBLICATION OF **"YOU MAY AS WELL EAT THE BOX"**. THE BOOK WAS AN EXPOSÉ OF CORPORATE ABUSE AND CORRUPTION WHICH DWELT ALMOST EXCLUSIVELY ON BOX SUBSIDIARIES. INDEED THE BOOK'S TITLE WAS GARNERED FROM EVIDENCE THAT SHOWED THAT MRS. HOPE'S KITCHEN PRODUCTS WERE NOT AS NUTRITIONAL AS THE CARDBOARD BOXES WHICH CONTAINED THEM! THE BOOK BECAME A MUCH DISCUSSED BEST SELLER AND MARKED THE BEGINNING OF A LONG PERIOD OF DECLINE FOR BOX.

HEADLINES DETAIL THE DECLINE...

BOLIGUAY NATIONALIZES
SOUTH AMERICAN SOCIALIST NATIONALIZES FOREIGN INTERESTS.

BOX TO LOSE A BUNDLE
MULTINATIONAL STOCK HITS NEW LOW

BOLIGUAY PRES: "CLOSE CALL."
ASSASSINATION ATTEMPT FOILED

BOX CHAIRMAN TRIGGERMAN?

BOX HEAD INDICTED!
62 COUNTS AGAINST WEBB

ELECTION RESULTS
SEN. SHURTZ OUT!
BOX TIES TOO TIGHT? VIRTUAL UNKNOWN WINS.

SEN. LEONARD, "DIVEST BOX NOW!"
NEW OHIO SENATOR WANTS BOX SHUT DOWN. CORRUPTION CITED

BOX HIT THE LOW-WATER MARK IN 1967 WHEN PRESTON WEBB AND SIX OTHER BOX OFFICERS WERE INDICTED ON VARIOUS CHARGES.

A NEW BEGINNING

JUST SHORT OF DECLARING BANKRUPTCY IN 1969, BOX INTERNATIONAL REORGANIZED AND EMERGED A YEAR LATER WITH AN ALTOGETHER NEW IMAGE AND A WIDELY PROCLAIMED 'ENLIGHTENED' MANAGEMENT.

WITHOUT SACRIFICING THE GREAT TASTE OF MRS. HOPES FOODS WHICH MILLIONS OF AMERICANS HAD COME TO LOVE, BOX ENDED CHARGES OF PACKAGING BEING MORE NUTRITIONAL THAN CONTENTS BY SIMPLY REPACKAGING THE FOOD STUFFS IN LESS NUTRITIONAL PLASTIC CONTAINERS.

IN A WIDELY PUBLICIZED DIVESTITURE MOVE, BOX MANAGEMENT ELECTED TO SELL OFF THE CORE OF BOX INDUSTRIES, THE AMMO SHELL & CASING DIVISION. MANAGEMENT, CITING HUMANISTIC REASONS AND GENERAL CONCERN FOR SMALL ANIMALS AND CHILDREN, SHREWDLY SHED OFF AN AGING UNPROFITABLE DIVISION AND AT THE SAME TIME WON WIDESPREAD MEDIA KUDOS AS A 'PROGRESSIVE, CONCERNED CORPORATION' AND ONE 'EAGER TO FACE THE CHALLENGE OF THE FUTURE'.

REVIEW

ESCAPE FROM THE MARKET WAS REALLY JUST A CONCERTED EFFORT BY GOVERNMENT TO CONTROL THE UNCERTAIN NATURE OF CAPITALISM. BEGINNING WITH THE ELECTION OF FRANKLIN ROOSEVELT WHO UTILIZED FISCAL POLICY AS STRESSED BY KEYNES, GOVERNMENT INTERVENTION RADICALLY ALTERED THE NATURE OF THE MARKET. LABOR WAS ENCOURAGED TO UNIONIZE, FARMERS WERE PAID **NOT** TO GROW CERTAIN CROPS, BANKERS AND CORPORATIONS FOUND THEMSELVES CLOSELY REGULATED AND FINALLY GOVERNMENT ASSURED THE EXISTENCE OF THOUSANDS OF JOBS BY MAKING MILITARY PURCHASES AND PUMPING BILLIONS OF DOLLARS INTO THE ECONOMY THROUGH SOCIAL PROGRAMS.

BUT, AS KEYNES DEVISED FISCAL POLICY, GOVERNMENT EXPENDITURES WERE MEANT ONLY TO AVERT UNEMPLOYMENT. ONCE AN ECONOMY HAD ACHIEVED A FULL EMPLOYMENT EQUILIBRIUM GOVERNMENT WAS TO STEP OUT SO THAT BUSINESS COULD EXPAND AND THEN FILL IN.
YOU CAN'T LEAVE NOW.
DON'T WORRY, SOMEONE ELSE WILL COME ALONG TO HIRE YOU.
THIS GUY JUST DON'T SEE IT LABOR'S WAY. HMM... WELL, WE'LL JUST HAVE TO ELECT SOMEONE ELSE WHO DOES.
BUT WHAT IF GOVERNMENT COULD NOT SCALE BACK ON PURCHASES AND HANDOUTS BECAUSE OF POLITICAL PRESSURE? THE ALTERNATIVE WAS TO RAISE TAXES OR RISK INFLATION.
I'M SORRY ABOUT THIS BUT I'VE GOT TO CUT BACK ON YOUR BUYING POWER.
YEA? WELL JUST WAIT TILL ELECTION TIME COMES ALONG FATSO.
IT SEEMED, NO MATTER WHAT, FISCAL POLICY WAS A ONE-WAY STREET WITHOUT EXITS.

AS GOVERNMENT EXPENDITURES CONTINUED TO EXPAND AND TAX REVENUES LAGGED BEHIND, AMERICANS BEGAN TO EXPERIENCE INFLATION.

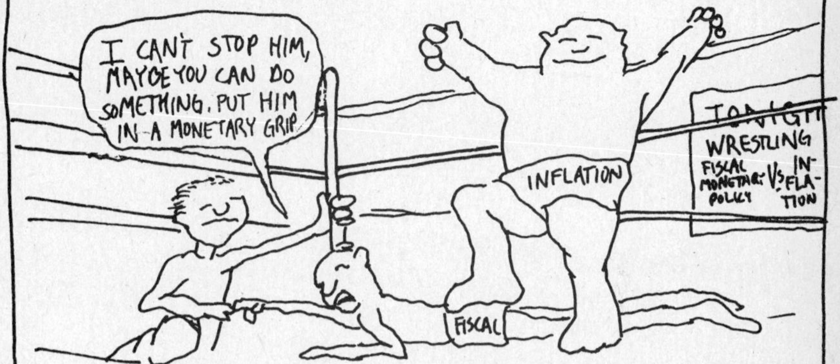

WHEN FISCAL POLICY PROVED NEARLY POWERLESS TO HALT INFLATION, GOVERNMENT TURNED TO MONETARY POLICY. THE FED RAISED INTEREST RATES, WHICH BROUGHT ON HIGHER UNEMPLOYMENT BUT DID LITTLE TO CURB INFLATION.* THE AMERICAN ECONOMY WAS IN A CRISIS SITUATION AS DESPERATE AS THE GREAT DEPRESSION. WITH THE PRESIDENTIAL ELECTION OF 1980 CAME A NEW ERA AND A NEW DIRECTION FOR THE AMERICAN ECONOMY.

* ECONOMISTS REFER TO AN ECONOMIC CONDITION WHERE BOTH INFLATION AND UNEMPLOYMENT PERSIST AS STAGFLATIO

PART 4
BACK TO THE
OPEN MARKET
OPEN MARKET

RONALD REAGAN. PROBABLY NOT A MAN AT ALL, PROBABLY A MYTH. AT LEAST THAT WOULD EXPLAIN HOW HE HAS MANAGED TO CUT SOCIAL PROGRAMS THAT HAD BENEFITTED NEARLY EVERY AMERICAN AND YET HIS POPULARITY HAS ONLY GOTTEN GREATER. HE HAS SPURRED THE COMPETITIVE NATURE OF THE AMERICAN ECONOMY THROUGH GOVERNMENT SPENDING CUTS, TAX CUTS AND A POLICY KNOWN AS SUPPLY-SIDE ECONOMICS.

REAGANOMICS: A SPECIAL BRAND OF FISCAL POLICY
FORGET THEM, LET'S TALK ABOUT THAT NEW MISSILE PROGRAM.
HANG IN THERE.
HEY! WHAT GIVES?
DESPITE THE OPPOSITION, REAGAN HAS SUCCESSFULLY ALTERED THE COURSE OF AMERICAN CAPITALISM. HE HAS SUCCESSFULLY OPPOSED UNIONIZED LABOR, SUBSIDIZED FARMERS AND NUMEROUS OTHER SPECIAL INTERESTS. HE HAS CUT BILLIONS OF DOLLARS IN GOVERNMENT AID TO ALMOST EVERY SECTOR OF THE ECONOMY EXCEPT DEFENSE. FURTHER, HE HAS IMPLEMENTED A TAX CUT AND PROPOSES EVEN MORE TAX REFORMS DESIGNED TO COMPLETELY REDIRECT AMERICAN TAX POLICY.
O.K.... SO THIS MYTHICAL POLITICIAN RONALD REAGAN HAS SOMEHOW CUT GOVERNMENT SPENDING AND MANAGED TO STAY IN OFFICE. BUT TAX CUTS?! HE SHOULD BE RAISING TAXES TO BALANCE THE BUDGET.
NO! HE'S CUTTING TAXES TO RAISE REVENUE BY SPURRING THE ECONOMY. IT'S CLASSIC SUPPLY SIDE ALL THE WAY
ALL THE WAY TO DISASTER.
AW, CLAM IT!

DEMAND-SIDE ECONOMICS
GO OUT THERE AND SPEND!
FISCAL POLICY, AS WE'VE NOTED, IS DESIGNED TO SPUR A SLUGGISH ECONOMY BY PUTTING MONEY INTO THE HANDS OF CONSUMERS. THE GOVERNMENT DOES THIS THROUGH PURCHASES OR DIRECT HANDOUTS.
DEMAND-SIDE ECONOMICS ⟹ IS SIMPLY PUMPING UP THE ECONOMY BY WAY OF THE CONSUMER. BUT WHAT ABOUT PUMPING UP THE ECONOMY BY WAY OF THE SUPPLIER..?
SUPPLY-SIDE ECONOMICS
RATHER THAN INCREASING DEMAND THROUGH GOVERNMENT HANDOUTS, SUPPLY SIDE OFFERS ADVANTAGES TO PRODUCERS WHO SUPPLY THE GOODS CONSUMERS DEMAND. THAT IS, GOVERNMENT OFFERS INCENTIVES (TAX BREAKS) TO PRODUCERS THAT ENCOURAGE THEM TO INVEST IN THE FORMATION OF CAPITAL GOODS.
KEEP THAT AND EXPAND.
TRICKLE DOWN
WHEN COMPANIES EXPAND, THEY HIRE MORE WORKERS. WHEN THESE NEW WORKERS SPEND THEIR PAY THE ADDITIONAL DEMAND CREATES NEW JOBS AND SO ON AND SO ON - DOWN THROUGH THE ENTIRE ECONOMY.

REVENUE SHARING

REVENUE SHARING WAS HEAVILY UTILIZED DURING THE 1970'S AS A MEANS OF HELPING STATE AND LOCAL GOVERNMENTS PROVIDE AND ADMINISTER PUBLIC SERVICES WITH FUNDS RAISED BY THE FEDERAL GOVERNMENT. WITH REAGANOMICS, REVENUE SHARING HAS TAKEN A BIT OF A TWIST...

EXPENDITURE SHARING

TAX POLICY
PROGRESSIVE VS FLAT
ONE OF THE BASIC PRECEPTS OF KEYNESIAN/FISCAL ECONOMICS IS THE PROGRESSIVE TAX POLICY. IN SHORT, AS AN INDIVIDUAL'S INCOME RISES, SO RISES THE PERCENTAGE OF INCOME THAT INDIVIDUAL MUST PAY IN TAXES.
SAY A PERSON MAKING $10,000 A YEAR PAYS 10% IN TAXES
"WHY SHOULD I PAY MORE? I DONT MAKE THAT MUCH.
AND A PERSON MAKING $50,000 A YEAR PAYS 50% IN TAXES.
$25,000 IN TAXES!!! WHY DO I DO IT?
THIS IS THE PROGRESSIVE INCOME TAX STRUCTURE. IT MAY SEEM FAIR THAT THOSE MAKING THE MOST MONEY SHOULD PAY THE MOST TAXES. HOWEVER, THE PROGRESSIVE TAX DOES IMPOSE SOME PROBLEMS.
PROBLEM NO. 1
INFLATION
AS WEVE SEEN, INFLATION PUSHES PEOPLE'S INCOMES INTO HIGHER TAX BRACKETS. IN EFFECT, TRYING TO STAY EVEN BECOMES A LOSING GAME.
PROBLEM NO. 2
"WHY SHOULD I WORK HARDER? A RAISE AND A PROMOTION WOULD ONLY INCREASE MY TAX RATE. SO AFTER PAYING TAXES ID MAKE LESS INCOME THAN I DO NOW."

ART LAFFER, A CONTEMPORARY AMERICAN ECONOMIST, ILLUSTRATED, IN GRAPH FORM, ONE OF REAGANOMICS' MORE POPULAR IDEAS, THAT IS, THAT AS AMERICAN TAXPAYERS ENTERED HIGHER TAX BRACKETS THEIR INCENTIVE TO EARN MORE DECLINED, THEREBY DIMINISHING POTENTIAL TAX REVENUE. THE SOLUTION, AS LAFFER AND OTHER REAGANITES SAW IT, WAS THE 'FLAT TAX.

WOULD A FLAT TAX RATE INCREASE GOVERNMENT REVENUES? WOULD PEOPLE ACTUALLY WORK MORE IF THEY HAD TO PAY LESS INCOME TAXES? WOULD COMPANIES PRODUCE MORE JUST BECAUSE OF TAX INCENTIVES?

BUT ONE THING IS CERTAIN. A CHANGE IN THE TAX STRUCTURE WOULD ALTER THE DIRECTION OF SAVINGS AND INVESTMENTS. AS IT IS, HIGH INCOME PEOPLE, THOSE WITH THE MOST AVAILABLE MONEY FOR SAVING AND INVESTING, ARE INCLINED TO PUT THEIR MONEY IN SO-CALLED 'TAX SHELTERS'. THESE INVESTMENTS ARE NOT TYPICALLY THE KIND THAT LEND THEMSELVES TO CAPITAL FORMATION. RATHER, SHELTERS ARE DESIGNED ONLY TO PROTECT INCOME FROM TAXES.

TRICKLE DOWN -VS- THE GREAT SOCIETY
IN THE NEVER ENDING WAR ON POVERTY
IF YOU COULD THINK OF POVERTY AS A KIND OF HUGE HOLE IN THE LANDSCAPE, THEN THE GREAT SOCIETY PROGRAMS OF THE...
1960'S WERE A FISCAL EFFORT TO FILL THAT HOLE WITH MONEY,..
...AND FLOAT THE POOR UP TO THE SURFACE.

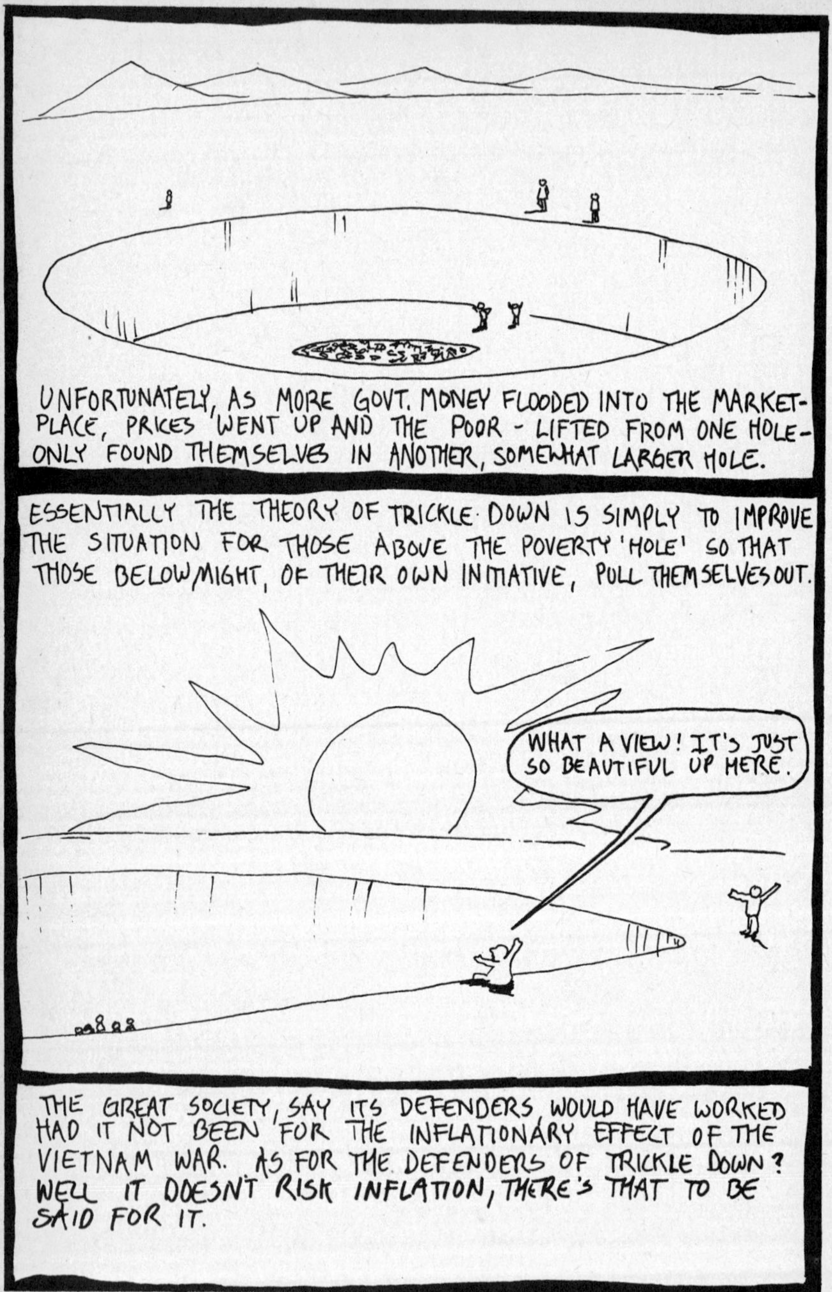
UNFORTUNATELY, AS MORE GOVT. MONEY FLOODED INTO THE MARKETPLACE, PRICES WENT UP AND THE POOR - LIFTED FROM ONE HOLE - ONLY FOUND THEMSELVES IN ANOTHER, SOMEWHAT LARGER HOLE.
ESSENTIALLY THE THEORY OF TRICKLE DOWN IS SIMPLY TO IMPROVE THE SITUATION FOR THOSE ABOVE THE POVERTY 'HOLE' SO THAT THOSE BELOW MIGHT, OF THEIR OWN INITIATIVE, PULL THEMSELVES OUT.
WHAT A VIEW! IT'S JUST SO BEAUTIFUL UP HERE.
THE GREAT SOCIETY, SAY ITS DEFENDERS, WOULD HAVE WORKED HAD IT NOT BEEN FOR THE INFLATIONARY EFFECT OF THE VIETNAM WAR. AS FOR THE DEFENDERS OF TRICKLE DOWN? WELL IT DOESN'T RISK INFLATION, THERE'S THAT TO BE SAID FOR IT.

REVIEW

WILL THE REAGAN-INSPIRED REEMPHASIS ON THE OPEN MARKET LAST? PROBABLY, FOR AWHILE ANYWAY, THEN THE MOOD OF THE COUNTRY WILL SURELY SWING ANOTHER WAY. THE GENERAL RULE IS THAT PEOPLE WANT WHATEVER IT IS THAT THEY DON'T HAVE. WHEN MONETARY STABILITY IS THE ORDER OF THE DAY PEOPLE ARE PRONE TO EASING CREDIT AND PROMOTING THE VERY CONDITIONS WHICH CAN LEAD TO COLLAPSE. AND IN TIMES OF FINANCIAL DISTRESS, FOLKS LONG FOR STABILITY EVEN AT THE PRICE OF GOVERNMENT INTERVENTION. BUT THEN THIS IS PROBABLY AS IT SHOULD BE. SO LONG AS CHANGE CAN BE BROUGHT ABOUT BY AN INFORMED, DEMOCRATIC SOCIETY THAT SOCIETY CAN ACHIEVE HEALTH AND PROSPERITY OVER THE LONG RUN.

PART 5

CLOSING DOWN THE OPEN MARKET AND THROWING AWAY THE KEY

UP TO NOW WE HAVE LOOKED AT THE VARIOUS WAYS IN WHICH PEOPLE HAVE COME TOGETHER TO SOLVE THEIR ECONOMIC PROBLEMS. WE HAVE SEEN THE CRUEL BUT EFFECTIVE **COMMAND** ECONOMY, THE SIMPLE BUT RIGID **TRADITIONAL** ECONOMY AND FINALLY THE DEVELOPMENT OF THE FLEXIBLE AND DYNAMIC **MARKET** ECONOMY. AND WE HAVE SEEN HOW THE MARKET ECONOMY INSTILLED IN PEOPLE THE PROFIT MOTIVE, WHICH GUIDED THEM TO SEEK, OWN AND AMASS LAND, MONEY AND CAPITAL. BUT WHAT ABOUT THOSE NOT SO MOTIVATED FOR PROFIT, THE WORKERS? THOSE WHOM KARL MARX CLAIMED CREATED ALL VALUE? COULD THERE NOT BE ANOTHER ECONOMIC STRUCTURE WHICH MIGHT BEST BENIFIT THEM?

ASSUMING, AS MARX DID, THAT ALL VALUE WAS CREATED BY LABOR ALONE, THEN HOW COULD YOU STRUCTURE AN ECONOMY THAT MIGHT BEST DIRECTLY BENEFIT LABOR. FIRST THERE WOULD BE **NO** PROFIT MOTIVE. AS MARX ONCE PUT IT SO WELL, "TO EACH ACCORDING TO HIS NEED, FROM EACH ACCORDING TO HIS ABILITY." BUT AS NICE AS THAT MAY SOUND, WHAT DOES IT ACTUALLY MEAN? WHO WOULD DETERMINE WHAT SOME-ONE NEEDED OR DIDN'T NEED? AND WHAT ABOUT SOMETHING THAT EVERYONE FELT THEY NEEDED BUT THERE JUST WASN'T ENOUGH TO GO AROUND? WHAT THEN? IN SHORT, HOW WOULD THE ECONOMY DECIDE WHO GOT WHAT AND WHY?

WELCOME TO CENTRAL PLANNING

WITHOUT THE PROFIT MECHANISM TO DIRECT THE PLACEMENT OF WORKERS AND MATERIALS, THE **NONMARKET** SOCIETY MUST CREATE SOME KIND OF CENTRAL COMMITTEE TO OVERSEE AND DIRECT EVERYTHING. THIS INCLUDES WHAT IS MADE, WHO MAKES IT, WHO WILL RECEIVE WHAT IS MADE AND ON AND ON AND ON. FOR EXAMPLE, THE TOTAL NUMBER OF TREES CUT FOR THE YEAR MUST BE PREDETERMINED, AND THE AMOUNT OF WOOD GOING TO THE VARIOUS INDUSTRIES THAT NEED LUMBER MUST BE KNOWN IN ADVANCE. OTHERWISE THERE COULD BE TOO MANY TOOTH-PICKS AND NOT ENOUGH HOUSES. THIS KIND OF CENTRAL PLANNING REQUIRES AN ENORMOUS AMOUNT OF COORDINATION, CO-OPERATION AND OFTEN ENFORCEMENT.

1917

TO UNDERSTAND HOW THE WORKER'S PARADISE OF MARX'S DREAMS CAME TO BE THE RIGID, CRUEL AND ALL-POWERFUL STATE THAT WE NOW KNOW TO BE COMMUNISM LETS LOOK BRIEFLY AT THE STORY OF THE SOVIET UNION.

1917. THIS WAS THE YEAR THAT THE PEOPLE OF RUSSIA SUCCESSFULLY REVOLTED AGAINST THEIR CZARIST RULERS. BUT AT THAT TIME IT WASN'T AT ALL CERTAIN WHAT KIND OF NEW GOVERNMENT WOULD TAKE POWER.

OF COURSE THERE WERE SOME COMMUNISTS THEN, LENIN BEING CHIEF AMONG THEM, BUT THE PROBLEM THEY FOUND, IN INCITING A COMMUNIST TAKEOVER, HAD TO DO WITH THE DIRE LACK OF INDUSTRIAL WORKERS. RUSSIA, AT THAT TIME, WAS LARGELY A FEUDAL SOCIETY WITH PEASANTS MAKING UP THE BULK OF THE POPULATION. THERE WERE FEW, IF ANY, CAPITALISTS TO OVERTHROW. SQUALID FACTORY CONDITIONS WERE AS YET UNKNOWN. INDEED, MARX HIMSELF, BEFORE HE DIED, DID NOT THINK RUSSIA A LIKELY PLACE FOR A COMMUNIST TAKEOVER, AT LEAST NOT UNTIL THE CAPITALIST FACTORY SYSTEM WAS WELL IN PLACE AND A FEW MILLION PEASANTS HAD BEEN DISPLACED AND THROWN INTO THE REGIMENTED FACTORY SYSTEM.

BUT FOR LENIN AND THE OTHER RUSSIAN COMMUNISTS THERE WAS NO POINT IN WAITING, POSSIBLY YEARS, FOR AN INDUSTRIAL PROLETARIAT TO COME ALONG, NOT WHEN THERE WAS REVOLUTION GOING ON ALL AROUND THEM. THUS, AS LENIN SAW IT, ALTER THE CONCEPT OF COMMUNISM A LITTLE BIT AND MAKE IT APPEALING TO PEASANTS AS WELL. THIS LENIN DID BY PROMISING LAND REFORM. THAT IS, BREAK UP THE HUGE ESTATES OF THE CZARIST NOBLES AND PARCEL OUT THE LAND TO THE PEASANTS WHO HAD WORKED IT FOR GENERATIONS. NEEDLESS TO SAY, THIS ENABLED LENIN TO GAIN WIDESPREAD SUPPORT AND BEFORE LONG HE AND HIS COMMUNIST BUDDIES WERE ABLE TO TAKE AND CONSOLIDATE POWER IN RUSSIA. ONCE IN POWER, LENIN DID AS HE PROMISED AND IN A SENSE HE CREATED A LARGE MIDDLE CLASS OF SMALL, INDEPENDENT FARMERS. FORMERLY PEASANTS, THESE FOLKS WERE WORKING HARD, SELLING THEIR GOODS, MAKING A SMALL PROFIT AND GENERALLY ENGAGING IN MARKET ACTIVITIES WITHIN A SO-CALLED COMMUNIST COUNTRY.
"WELL IF THE SHOE FITS, WEAR IT. IF IT DOESN'T FIT, WEAR IT ANYWAY."
WELL OKAY, THIS MAY NOT BE COMMUNISM PER SE, BUT IT TAKES TIME AND NO ONE'S EVER DONE IT BEFORE. JUST GIVE US SOME TIME TO WORK IT ALL OUT.
AT WHICH POINT LENIN DROPPED DEAD.

LENIN WAS SUCCEEDED BY JOSEPH STALIN, A MAN WHO CLEARLY HAD HIS OWN IDEAS ABOUT WHAT COMMUNISM WAS ALL ABOUT AND HOW TO GO ABOUT ACHIEVING IT. FIRST OF ALL, STALIN WANTED TO INDUSTRIALIZE THE SOVIET UNION. NOW AS WE KNOW, THE INDUSTRIAL PROCESS IS NEVER AN EASY ONE BUT FOR RUSSIANS UNDER STALIN IT WOULD TAKE ON A WHOLE NEW MEANING. FIRST OF ALL THE DIFFICULTY IN INDUSTRIALIZING IS THAT IT REQUIRES A SOCIETY TO ABSTAIN FROM PRESENT CONSUMPTION OF THE THINGS IT WANTS SO THAT WORKERS CAN BE GIVEN THE TASK OF CAPITAL FORMATION. THAT IS, BUILDING THE VERY FACTORIES AND MACHINERY THAT ARE USED TO BUILD THE INDUSTRIAL TOOLS THAT SO ENHANCE WORKER PRODUCTIVITY.

NOW, IN ACTUAL TERMS, THIS MEANT THAT ALL THOSE MIDDLE CLASS FARMERS COULD NOT GO OUT AND SELL THEIR GOODS FOR MARKET VALUE AND THEN BUY THE THINGS THEY WANTED. NO, INSTEAD THEY WERE TO SELL THEIR FARM PRODUCTS CHEAPLY TO THE GOVERNMENT SO THE GOVERNMENT COULD FEED THE MANY WORKERS INVOLVED IN CAPITAL FORMATION PROJECTS. SADLY, THE RUSSIAN FARMERS WEREN'T KEEN ON THE IDEA AND CONSEQUENTLY STALIN WASNT KEEN ON THEM. HIS SOLUTION?

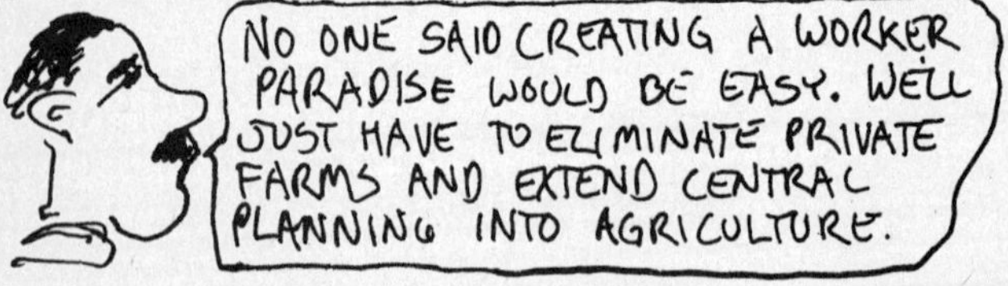

IN TRUTH, STALIN DID MORE THAN ELIMINATE PRIVATE FARMS, HE ELIMINATED ABOUT 5 MILLION FARMERS ALONG THE WAY AND ANYONE ELSE WHO QUESTIONED HIS INTERPRETATION OF COMMUNISM.

BY EXERTING HIS WILL OVER SOVIET SOCIETY, STALIN NECESSITATED THE POLICE STATE WHICH HAS REMAINED THE DOMINANT FACTOR IN SUSTAINING THE SO-CALLED COMMUNIST GOVERNMENT IN RUSSIA TODAY. WHILE A POLICE STATE ENVIRONMENT POSES CERTAIN SOCIAL PROBLEMS THE FACT REMAINS THAT RUSSIA ACHIEVED INDUSTRIALIZATION IN RECORD TIME AND CONTINUES TO POST TECHNOLOGICAL ADVANCEMENTS THAT COMPARE FAVORABLY TO THE 'PROFIT-MOTIVATED' WESTERN NATIONS.

ON THE FARM WITH THE PROFIT MOTIVE

WHILE SOME ASPECTS OF A LARGE AND ANONYMOUS AMERICAN CORPORATION MAY BE SIMILIAR TO A LARGE STATE-OWNED SOVIET CONCERN, THERE ARE IMPORTANT AND OBVIOUS DIFFERENCES WHEN IT COMES TO COMPARING AMERICAN FARMERS WITH THEIR COMMUNIST COUNTERPARTS WORKING STATE-OWNED FARM COOPERATIVES. THE SOVIET UNION MUST REALIZE THIS EVERY YEAR WHEN IT MUST IMPORT MILLIONS OF TONS OF GRAIN DESPITE ITS VAST AND FERTILE FARMLAND. AND LATELY, CHINA TOO HAS COME TO THE CONCLUSION THAT MARKET INCENTIVES (PROFIT) ARE NEEDED TO INCREASE FARM OUTPUT. BUT WHY IS THAT SO?

THE FUTURE OF COMMUNISM

CAPITALISM, DESPITE LONG-HERALDED PREDICTIONS OF ITS DEMISE, IS STILL WITH US AND THRIVING.

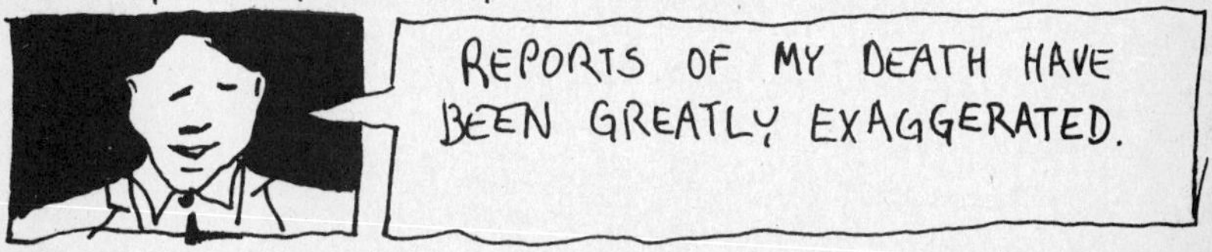

BUT IS COMMUNISM, WHICH RULES OVER NEARLY HALF THE WORLD'S POPULATION, EXPERIENCING A DECLINE? OR COULD A MARXIST STYLE GOVERNMENT IN NICARAGUA INFLUENCE FURTHER COMMUNIST SUCCESSES IN SOUTH AND CENTRAL AMERICA? THE ANSWER TO THIS QUESTION GOES BACK AGAIN TO LAND AND FARMERS AND THE LAND REFORMS OF THE SOVIET REVOLUTION. CLEARLY, THE MARXIST GOVERNMENT IN NICARAGUA IS POPULAR BECAUSE THEY HAVE INSTIGATED SIMILAR LAND REFORMS. PEASANTS HAVE BEEN GIVEN OWNERSHIP OF SMALL TRACTS OF LAND FROM FORMER ESTATES WHERE THEY HAD WORKED AS PEASANTS. BUT WILL THESE LAND REFORMS REMAIN INTACT? OR WILL THE COMMUNISTS EXERT BRUTE FORCE, AS IN RUSSIA AND CHINA, TO IMPOSE THEIR WILL AND SET UP THE COMMAND ECONOMY THAT COMMUNISM ULTIMATELY RESEMBLES? THE QUESTION BECOMES A POLITICAL ONE AND PROBABLY FOR THAT REASON COMMUNISM HAS YET TO TAKE ON, FOR ANY EXTENSIVE PERIOD, THE FEATURES OF A DEMOCRACY. AND THEREIN LIES A VERY DANGEROUS BUT REAL PROBLEM FOR PEOPLE OF UNDEVELOPED NATIONS THINKING OF TURNING TO COMMUNISM. ONCE COMMUNIST RULERS HAVE EXERTED AUTHORITARIAN CONTROL OVER THE MARKET THEY WILL PROBABLY (AS HISTORY HAS SHOWN) ABOLISH ANY SEMBLANCE OF DEMOCRACY.

PART 6
THE WORLD OF PERFECT COMPETITION
Economics in the Classroom

ALONG ABOUT THE TIME THAT KARL MARX WAS MAKING HIS LONG-WINDED POSTULATIONS OF HOW VALUE WAS DETERMINED BY LABOR ALONE, OTHER ECONOMISTS WERE PUTTING FORWARD THE NOTION THAT PERHAPS VALUE WASN'T SO MUCH WHAT WENT INTO A GOOD AS WHAT WAS TO BE GOTTEN OUT OF IT. TRAVELLING FURTHER DOWN THIS LINE OF THOUGHT GOT ECONOMISTS WONDERING...

VERY LIKELY SO. THE IDEA WAS CALLED MARGINALISM, AND IT PRESENTED THE POSSIBILITY THAT VALUE AND WEALTH WERE NOT SO MUCH THE PRODUCTS OF LAND OR LABOR OR CHESTS OF GOLD BUT MORE THE EVER SHIFTING, EVER CHANGING WANTS AND NEEDS OF PEOPLE. WELL, AS IT IS SOMETIMES SAID, "ANYTHING SO PLAINLY OBVIOUS IS FAIR GAME FOR CONFUSION!" WHICH MAY EXPLAIN WHY ECONOMICS, WITH ITS ENDLESS AND MYSTICAL THEORIES, PRINCIPLES, GRAPHS AND CURVES, HAS BEFUDDLED SO MANY SO NEEDLESSLY. BUT, BE THAT AS IT MAY, HOPEFULLY IN THESE FINAL PAGES WE CAN UNSCRAMBLE, AND FIND APPLICATION FOR, THE MOST COMMONLY ENCOUNTERED CONCEPTS OF TEXTBOOK ECONOMICS NO MATTER HOW NEVER-NEVER WORLD THEY MAY SEEM.

CHOICE & SCARCITY

IF EVERYTHING WERE PLENTIFUL IN THE WORLD, THERE WOULD, NO DOUBT, BE A SCARCITY OF ECONOMISTS. THEN THEY COULD STUDY THEMSELVES. BECAUSE ECONOMICS IS, SIMPLY, THE STUDY OF CHOICE AND SCARCITY.

SCARCITY IS SIMPLY THE RELATIONSHIP BETWEEN AVAILABILITY AND DESIRABILITY.

THEREFORE AN ECONOMIST WOULD HAVE TO DESCRIBE SUSAN AS A SCARCE PROSPECT FOR A DATE ON SATURDAY NIGHT, WHILE JEWEL AND THE GIRLS, SADLY, WOULD NOT FIT THAT DESCRIPTION. INDEED, AVAILABLE DATES ARE PLENTIFUL, AND YET FOR A GUY WANTING A **DESIRABLE** DATE, THERE WOULD BE SCARCITY.

THE LAW OF SUPPLY & DEMAND

ACTUALLY IT IS NOT YET LAW IN ANYONES BOOK. IN FACT, IN THE REAL WORLD (NOT APPLICABLE HERE) VIOLATIONS OCCUR EVERY DAY ON THE ORDER OF GOVERNMENT REGULATIONS, LARGE CORPORATIONS, UNIONS AND SUCH. ANYWAY, SUPPLY AND DEMAND IS THAT ASPECT OF ECONOMICS WHICH GRAPHS OUT THE RELATIONSHIP BETWEEN AVAILABILITY AND DESIRABILITY.

WHAT MAKES SUSAN SO DESIRABLE YET NOT QUITE AVAILABLE? BOB AND HIS FRIENDS, THAT'S WHAT. SINCE SUSAN IS IN SUCH SHORT SUPPLY AND AT THE SAME TIME IN SUCH STRONG DEMAND SHE MAY, IN THE MANNER OF A MONOPOLIST,* NAME HER PRICE. MEANING THAT BOB AND THE BOYS MUST BID AGAINST EACH OTHER, DRIVING UP THE PRICE OF A DATE (FROM SAY EARLY OFFERS OF A PIZZA TO A WINNING OFFER OF, SAY, DINNER AT A FANCY RESTAURANT AND A CONCERT) UNTIL ONLY ONE IS LEFT WILLING TO PAY THE PRICE.

*A MONOPOLIST IS A SUPPLIER WHO FACES NO COMPETITION. AN OLIGOPOLIST IS A SUPPLIER WHO FACES VERY FEW OR MUCH SMALLER COMPETITORS. STRICTLY SPEAKING, SUSAN IS AN OLIGOPOLIST AS IS G.M. OR I.B.M.

A PRIMER CONCERNING GRAPHS & CURVES

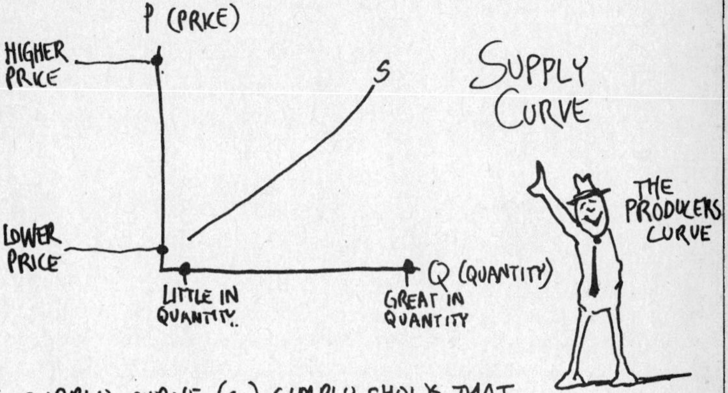

THE SUPPLY CURVE (S) SIMPLY SHOWS THAT, AS THE PRICE OF A GOOD RISES, MORE SUPPLIES OF THAT GOOD BECOME AVAILABLE (AND VICE VERSA).

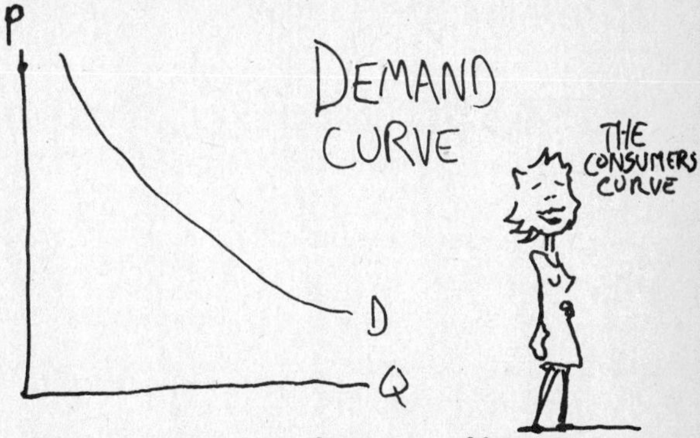

UTILIZING THE SAME RELATIONSHIP BETWEEN PRICE AND QUANTITY, THE DEMAND CURVE (D) MOVES IN A DIFFERENT DIRECTION SHOWING THAT AS THE PRICE OF A GOOD FALLS CONSUMERS OF THAT GOOD WILL DEMAND MORE (AND VICE VERSA).

CHOICES

NOTHING COULD BE MORE ESSENTIAL TO THE STUDY OF ECONOMICS THAN CHOICE. THINK OF SCARCITY AS THE TRACK AND CHOICE AS THE TRAIN.

BOB AND THE BOYS WERE ALL WILLING TO SPARE THE PRICE OF A PIZZA TO WIN A DATE WITH SUSAN. BUT, AT SOME PRICE, EACH ONE MAKES THE CHOICE TO DO SOMETHING ELSE. AS A WELL-SCHOOLED ECONOMIST MIGHT SAY, "WHEN WE THINK THAT WE HAVE CHOSEN TO DO A THING, WE HAVE ACTUALLY CHOSEN NOT TO DO SOMETHING ELSE." AS TURNED AROUND AS THIS LOGIC MAY SEEM, IT IS TRUE AND APPLIES TO EVERYONE, TO PRODUCERS AND CONSUMERS, TO INDIVIDUALS AND COUNTRIES. WHEN A NATION CHOOSES TO INCREASE MILITARY SPENDING IT MUST DECREASE SOCIAL SPENDING (THEORETICALLY). WHEN THE PRICE OF A GOOD RISES TOO HIGH WE WILL CHOOSE TO BUY LESS. WHY? BECAUSE PAYING THE HIGHER PRICE WILL MEAN LOSING THE OPPORTUNITY TO BUY SOMETHING ELSE. ECONOMISTS REFER TO THIS ASTOUNDING PERCEPTION AS...

OPPORTUNITY COSTS

OPPORTUNITY COSTS ARE LOST BY BOTH PRODUCERS AND CONSUMERS. OBVIOUS AS IT SEEMS, EVERY TIME YOU BUY SOMETHING YOU MISS THE OPPORTUNITY TO BUY SOMETHING ELSE.

WANTING TO SELL THE HAT, THE SALESMAN RECOGNIZED THAT THE OPPORTUNITY MISSED (SCARF) WAS GREATER, THEREFORE HE INGENIOUSLY REMOVED THE COST OF THE HAT ALTOGETHER.

GETTING TO KNOW YOUR DEMAND CURVE

DEMAND FOR MOST THINGS STAYS FAIRLY CONSTANT. FOR EXAMPLE, YOU EITHER EAT MEAT OR YOU DON'T. BUT WHAT WOULD HAPPEN TO YOUR DEMAND FOR BEEF IF THE PRICE WENT TOO HIGH? YOU WOULD PROBABLY BUY LESS BEEF AND POSSIBLY BUY MORE FISH OR CHICKEN. IN THIS CASE BEEF IS EASILY SUBSTITUTED FOR BY SOME OTHER MEAT. TO A DEGREE, EVERYTHING HAS SUBSTITUTES, IT'S JUST THAT SOME THINGS HAVE BETTER SUBSTITUTES THAN OTHERS. FOR INSTANCE, WE KNOW THAT MARGARINE IS A GOOD SUBSTITUTE FOR BUTTER, BUT WHAT IS A GOOD SUBSTITUTE FOR GASOLINE? CERTAINLY NOT MAZOLA. ECONOMISTS CAN DETERMINE THE AVAILABILITY OF SUBSTITUTES FOR A PARTICULAR GOOD BY MEASURING THE SLOPE OF THAT GOOD'S DEMAND CURVE. THE SLOPE OF THE DEMAND CURVE FOR GASOLINE DIFFERS SHARPLY FROM THE SLOPE OF THE CURVE FOR BEEF. ECONOMISTS HAVE DEVELOPED THEIR OWN UNIQUE TERMINOLOGY FOR DISCUSSING THE VARYING SLOPES OF DIFFERENT DEMAND CURVES...

ELASTICITY OF DEMAND

EVERY DEMAND CURVE HAS WHAT ECONOMISTS CALL 'ELASTICITY. THE ELASTICITY OF DEMAND FOR A PARTICULAR GOOD TELLS A GREAT DEAL ABOUT THE AVAILABILITY OF CHOICES OR SUBSTITUTES FOR THAT GOOD. GASOLINE IS OFTEN CITED AS A FINE EXAMPLE OF DEMAND CURVE '**IN**ELASTICITY LET'S TAKE A LOOK AT AN EXAMPLE OF A HIGHLY **ELASTIC** DEMAND CURVE.

PEPPE IS GOING TO DISCOVER THAT NOT ONLY IS HIS PEPPERONI PIZZA TASTY, IT'S HIGHLY ELASTIC.

GRAPHING ELASTICITY BY MEASURING THE SLOPE OF THE DEMAND CURVE

IN A PERFECTLY COMPETITIVE MARKET THE SLOPE OF THE DEMAND CURVE IS 45°. WHY? BECAUSE ANY PERCENTAGE CHANGE IN THE PRICE OF A GOOD WILL MATCH EXACTLY THE PERCENTAGE CHANGE IN THE QUANTITY DEMANDED OF THAT GOOD. HENCE A 10% DECREASE IN PRICE WOULD RESULT IN A 10% INCREASE IN QUANTITY DEMANDED.

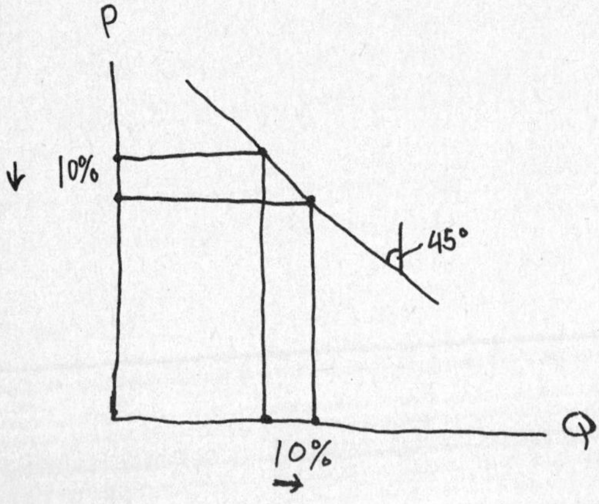

WILL PEPPE DOUBLE HIS REVENUE BY DOUBLING THE PRICE OF HIS PEPPERONI PIZZA? NOT A CHANCE. ASSUMING THE DEMAND ELASTICITY ABOVE HE WOULD AT BEST BREAK EVEN. THAT IS, BY DOUBLING HIS PRICE HE WOULD CUT HIS SALES IN HALF. HOWEVER, CHANCES ARE BETTER THAN EVEN THAT NOT EVEN HALF OF PEPPE'S CUSTOMERS WOULD BE WILLING TO PAY SUCH HIGH PRICES. SADLY, PEPPE'S PEPPERONI PIZZA FACES WHAT ECONOMISTS WOULD CALL A HIGLY ELASTIC DEMAND CURVE. THAT IS, A PERCENTAGE CHANGE IN PRICE WOULD RESULT IN A SIGNIFICANTLY GREATER PERCENTAGE CHANGE IN QUANTITY DEMANDED. PRACTICALLY SPEAKING, PEPPE WILL LOSE A LOT OF MONEY.

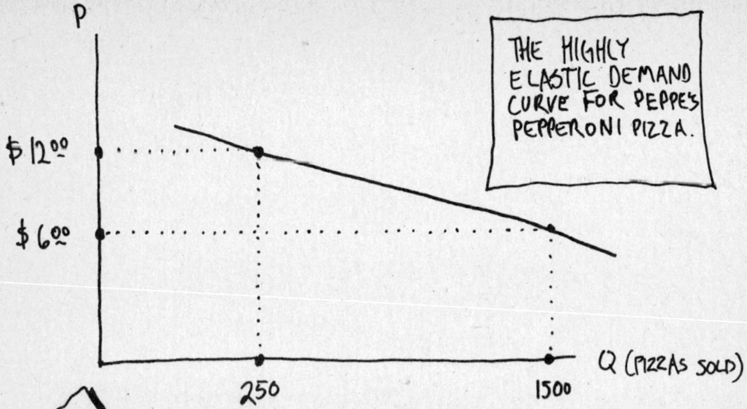

LET'S SAY IN ONE WEEK 1500 PEOPLE BOUGHT PEPPE'S PEPPERONI PIZZA AT $6.00 PER PIZZA. WHEN PEPPE DOUBLES HIS PRICE, ONLY A FRACTION (ONE IN SIX) OF HIS CUSTOMERS WILL CONTINUE TO BUY HIS PEPPERONI PIZZA. IF IT'S ANY COMFORT TO PEPPE, MOST GOODS FACE HIGHLY ELASTIC DEMAND CURVES BECAUSE GOOD SUBSTITUTES ABOUND. BUT WHAT ABOUT GASOLINE? A COMMODITY THAT DOESN'T READILY HAVE SUBSTITUTES?

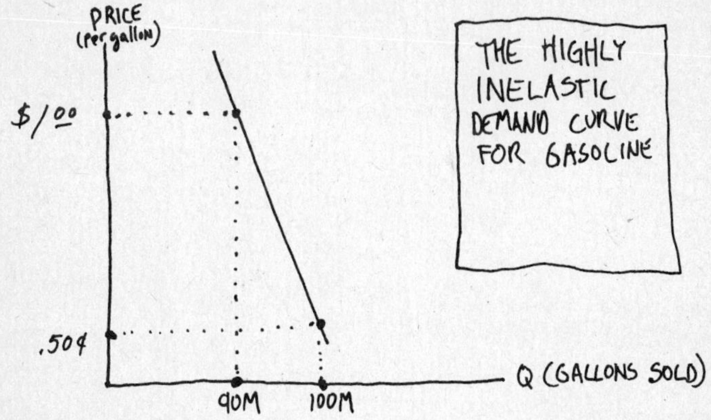

SINCE MANY PEOPLE DEPEND HEAVILY ON GASOLINE AND THE ONLY SIMPLE ALTERNATIVE IS CUTTING BACK ON CONSUMPTION, WHICH MANY CAN'T DO, GASOLINE HAS A VERY INELASTIC DEMAND CURVE. THAT IS, A PERCENTAGE CHANGE IN PRICE WILL BE MUCH GREATER THAN ANY RESULTING PERCENTAGE CHANGE IN QUANTITY DEMANDED.

COMPETITION. IT WAS COMPETITION AMONG BOB AND HIS FRIENDS THAT PUSHED THE PRICE OF A DATE WITH SUSAN UP AND UP. JUST AS IT WAS COMPETITION FROM OTHER PIZZA PARLORS THAT PREVENTED PEPPE FROM DOUBLING HIS PROFITS BY MERELY DOUBLING THE PRICE OF HIS PEPPERONI PIZZA.

IT'S CALLED PRICE EQUILIBRIUM ('E' ON THE CHARTS) AND IT REPRESENTS THAT HAPPY PLACE WHERE SUPPLY AND DEMAND MEET. THAT IS, WHERE CONSUMERS ARE WILLING TO PURCHASE GOODS AT PRICES THAT PRODUCERS ARE WILLING TO SUPPLY.

PARDON ME, BUT I WAS JUST WONDERING IF YOU WOULD INDULGE ME IN A LITTLE HYPOTHETICAL SWEET NOTHING?
MY LUCK TO SIT NEXT TO AN ECONOMIST
HOW THE WEST WAS REALLY WON
OR "CHALK FIGHT AT THE S&D CURVE
MEET THE SHERIFF OF THE TOWN OF PRICE EQUILIBRIUM.
"MA'AM... FOLKS. I AIN'T LOOKING FOR NO TROUBLE. — I JUST WANNA KEEP THE 'DERN PEACE."
E
I WELCOME YOU GOOD FOLKS TO COME A'CALLING. YOU'LL FIND OUR PEACEFUL LITTLE TOWN SITUATED AT THE CROSSROADS OF DEMAND PIKE AND SUPPLY TRAIL.
SUPPLY TRAIL
DEMAND PIKE

"TAINT BUT ONE LAW IN THESE HERE PARTS AND I INTEND TO KEEP IT!"
MEANWHILE, JUST NORTH OF TOWN COME A THUNDERING HERD...
"SHERIFF! SHERIFF!"
"WHAT IS IT BOY?"
"I SEEN A GANG OF CONSUMERS A-HOOT'N AND HOLLERIN' AND RIDIN' STRAIGHT FER TOWN!"
"THE CONSUMER GANG, HUH? WELL I RECK'N THEM BOY'S IS COME LOOKING TO TAKE ADVANTAGE OF OUR'N LOW PRICED GOODS AND SERVICES."
"KNOW WHAT THAT'LL MEAN, BOY?"
"I SPECK PRICES IS SURE TO GO UP... MEANING ME AND MA'S DRY GOODS STORE'LL DO RIGHT FINE."
"FINE? SHORN. BUT FOR A MIGHTY BRIEF SPELL."
"HUH?"
FOLKS'LL PROFIT RIGHT FINE. SO FINE IN FACT THAT PRODUCERS FROM ALL OVER THE TERRITORY'LL FLOCK DOWN ON THIS TOWN LIKE BUZZARDS. AND THEY'LL BE BRINGING GOODS TO SELL AND DO YOU KNOW WHAT THAT'LL MEAN, BOY?

"...OVERSUPPLY, PRICES'LL HAVE TO COME DOWN."
"THAT'S RIGHT. YOUR MA AND A LOT OF OTHER FOLKS MIGHT'N BE ABLE TO COMPETE. QUITE A FEW WOULD GO FLAT BUST."
"GOLLY, SHERIFF, WE JUST GOTTA DO SOMETHING. POST A PRICE FREEZE 'FORN' THEM PRODUCERS GET HERE, THEN WE'LL REGULATE!"
"WHOA! HOLD ON THERE, BOY. YOU WATCH WHAT YOU'RE SAYING."
E
"THAT BE AGAIN' THE LAW! BESIDE WHICH THERE'D BE NO CALL FOR IT. ONCE THE DUST CLEARED I 'SPECT THERE MIGHT BE A FEW NEW FACES A-TENDING THE STORES BUT PRICES WOULD SETTLE JUST LIKE THEY IS NOW AND I'D HAVE DONE MY JOB AND NOT HAVE TO HANG NO NE."
NOT BAD. BUT WHAT EVER HAPPENED TO THE LITTLE BOY AND HIS MOTHER?
BITTER OVER LOSING THEIR INEFFECIENT DRY GOODS STORE THEY JOINED UP WITH THE OUT-LAW 'MARX-ENGELS' GANG. THEY WERE LAST SEEN SOUTH OF THE BORDER CROSSING INTO CENTRAL AMERICA.

DEFYING THE LAW of S.&D.

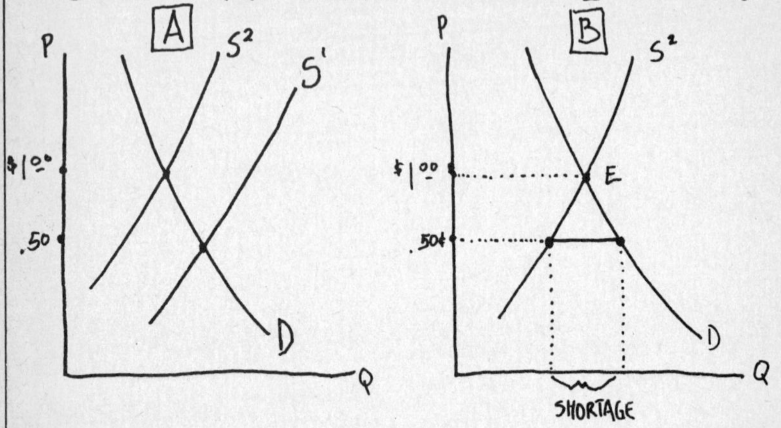

LET'S SAY THAT OIL PRODUCERS DECIDE TO REDUCE THE OVERALL SUPPLY OF OIL (FIG A: $S^1 \rightarrow S^2$). WITH AN INELASTIC CURVE DEMAND DROPS LESS THAN THE RISE IN PRICE. THE AMERICAN GOVERNMENT DECIDES TO FIX THE PRICE BY LAW AT THE OLD LEVEL OF 50¢ PER GALLON. THE RESULT IS A **SHORTAGE**. THAT IS, QUANTITY DEMANDED EXCEEDS QUANTITY SUPPLIED. IN SUCH CASES, PEOPLE END UP PAYING IN ANOTHER FORM. THE LONG GAS LINES OF THE 1970'S ARE A GOOD EXAMPLE OF SHORTAGE-PRICE SUBSTITUTION.

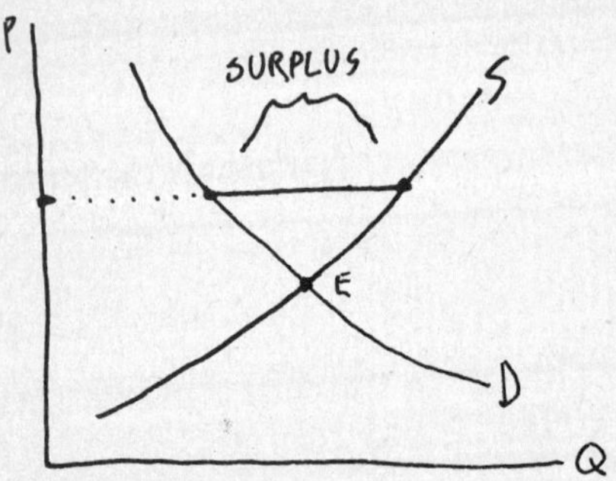

GOVERNMENT FARM PRICE SUPPORTS OFTEN RESULT IN **SURPLUS**. THAT IS, QUANTITY SUPPLIED EXCEEDS QUANTITY DEMANDED. A GOOD EXAMPLE IS THE FREQUENT SURPLUS OF... SAY CHEESE.

AT THE MARGIN

WHENEVER ECONOMIC DECISIONS ARE MADE, THEY ARE MADE AT THE MARGIN. THAT IS, DECISIONS ARE MADE BY CONSIDERING WHAT THE ADDITIONAL OR **MARGINAL** GAIN OR COST OF SUCH A DECISION WILL BE IN COMPARISON TO OTHER AVAILABLE CHOICES. DETERMINING THE **COMPARATIVE ADVANTAGE** OF ONE DECISION OVER ANOTHER IS THE BEST WAY FOR INDIVIDUALS, COMPANIES, EVEN NATIONS, TO MAKE CHOICES.

NOW LET'S GO BACK TO THAT HAPPY DAY WHEN PEPPE WAS SELLING 1500 PEPPERONI PIZZAS A WEEK FOR $6.00.

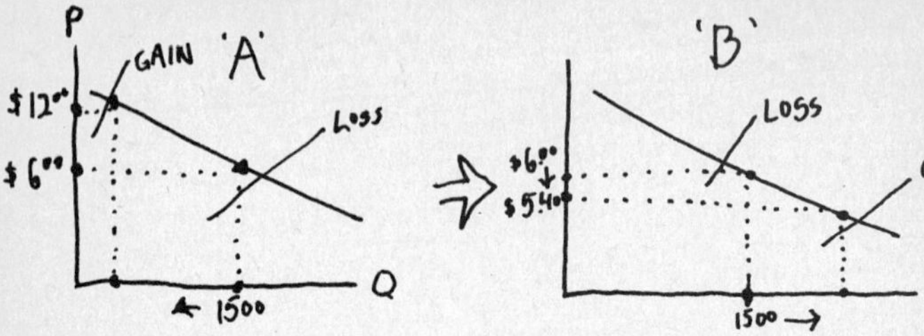

WHEN PEPPE RAISED HIS PRICE (FIG 'A') HE DISCOVERED THAT HIS GAIN FROM SELLING AT A HIGHER PRICE WAS FAR OUTSTRIPPED BY HIS LOSS IN QUANTITY DEMANDED. NOW LET'S SAY PEPPE DECIDES TO LOWER HIS PRICE 10%. IS IT POSSIBLE THAT HIS GAIN FROM SELLING MORE PIZZA (QUANTITY DEMANDED) WILL OUTSTRIP HIS LOSS FROM SELLING AT A LOWER PRICE?

PEPPE FIGURES UP ALL OF HIS COSTS IN MAKING 1500 PEPPERONI PIZZAS IN ONE WEEK AND HE COMES UP WITH A FIGURE OF $7875.00, OR AN AVERAGE COST PER PIZZA OF $5.25. WHAT WOULD IT COST PEPPE TO MAKE ONE MORE PIZZA? ANOTHER $5.25? NO! MOST OF PEPPE'S COSTS IN MAKING 1500 PIZZAS ARE FIXED COSTS (RENT, EQUIPMENT, LOAN PAYMENT, ETC.) AND WILL NOT INCREASE WHETHER PEPPE SELLS 1500 PIZZAS OR 1501. THEREFORE HIS ADDITIONAL OR MARGINAL COST OF MAKING ONE MORE PIZZA WILL REFECT ONLY MINOR COSTS, A BIT MORE FLOUR, SAUCE, PEPPERONI AND THE LIKE.

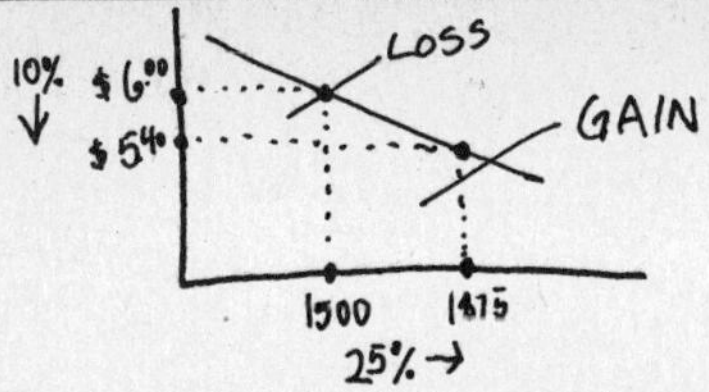

MARGINAL REVENUE WILL BE GAIN LESS LOSS.

BY LOWERING THE PRICE OF THIS PEPPERONI PIZZA 10% WE CALCULATE FROM THE SLOPE OF HIS DEMAND CURVE THAT QUANTITY DEMANDED WILL INCREASE 25%. MEANING HE WILL SELL 375 MORE PIZZAS. SO NOW PEPPE FIGURES UP WHAT IT WILL COST HIM TO MAKE AN ADDITIONAL 375 PEPPERONI PIZZAS, AND DETERMINES A FIGURE OF $125.00.

MARGINAL REVENUE

THE QUESTION PEPPE WANTS ANSWERED IS WILL HE MAKE GREATER PROFITS (PROFIT IS REVENUE LESS COST) BY LOWERING HIS PRICE AND SELLING MORE PIZZA? FIRST, CONSIDER HIS LOSSES PEPPE WAS SELLING 1500 PIZZAS AT $6.00 A PIZZA WHICH COST HIM $5.25 TO MAKE. HIS PROFIT WAS 75¢ A PIZZA FOR A TOTAL PROFIT OF $1,125.00. NOW WE'RE ASKING HIM TO LOWER HIS PRICE FROM $6.00 TO $5.40, MEANING HIS PROFIT PER PIZZA WILL DROP FROM 75¢ TO 15¢. THAT IS, HIS PROFIT FROM SELLING THE FIRST 1500 PIZZAS WILL DROP $900.00 TO $225.00.

BY SELLING HIS PEPPERONI PIZZA FOR 10% LESS IN PRICE PEPPE WILL SELL AN ADDITIONAL 375 PIZZAS. WILL THESE ADDITIONAL SALES MAKE UP FOR HIS LOSSES? FIRST REMEMBER THAT HIS MARGINAL COST FOR MAKING 375 MORE PIZZAS IS ONLY $125.00 OR AN AVERAGE MARGINAL COST OF ABOUT 33¢ A PIZZA. CONSIDERING THAT HE CAN SELL THOSE 375 PIZZAS FOR $5.40 EACH, YOU'D HAVE TO AGREE THAT PEPPE WILL ENJOY A SUBSTANTIAL MARGINAL PROFIT ON THOSE PIZZAS. BUT, WILL IT BE ENOUGH?

ORIGINAL REVENUE →	1500 x $5.40 →	$8100.00
MARGINAL REVENUE →	375 x $5.40 →	2025.00
TOTAL REVENUES →		$10,125.00
ORIGINAL COSTS →	1500 x $5.25 →	$ 7875.00
MARGINAL COSTS →	375 x $0.33⅓ →	$ 125.00
LOSS FROM NOT SELLING 1500 PIZZAS FOR $6.00 →	1500 x $0.60 →	$ 900.00
TOTAL COSTS →		$8900.00
PROFIT AT OLD PRICE (1500 x $0.75) →		$1,125.00
MARGINAL PROFIT →		$1,225.00

CONCLUSION

IS IT TO PEPPE'S ADVANTAGE TO MAKE THE ADDITIONAL PIZZAS? CERTAINLY THE MARGINAL COSTS OF MAKING THE ADDITIONAL PIZZAS SUGGEST THAT IT IS. HOWEVER PEPPE IS QUITE CORRECT TO QUESTION THE ADDITIONAL WORKLOAD IN COMPARISON TO THE ADDITIONAL OR MARGINAL REVENUE. BUT THEN THESE ARE THE QUESTIONS THAT COMPRISE THE ESSENCE OF WHAT ECONOMIC INQUIRY IS ALL ABOUT. PEOPLE MAKING CHOICES – WEIGHING THE COMPARATIVE ADVANTAGE OF ONE CHOICE OVER ANOTHER ~ CONSIDERING WHAT WILL BE LOST ON THE ONE HAND AND WHAT WILL BE GAINED ON THE OTHER. IN THE END IT IS THE VERY AVAILABILITY OF CHOICES THAT DETERMINES PROSPERITY. IN A SENSE, POVERTY IS MERELY THE ABSENCE OF CHOICE. A POOR MAN, ONLY FROM LACK OF MONEY, HAS FEW AVAILABLE OPTIONS. A PROSPEROUS SOCIETY IS ONE WHOSE MEMBERS CREATE A VAST ARRAY OF CHOICES AS EACH MEMBER PURSUES AND OFFERS THAT SKILL IN WHICH THEY BELIEVE THEY HOLD A COMPARATIVE ADVANTAGE.